The Boundaries of Technique

STUDIES IN ETHICS AND ECONOMICS

Series Editor
Samuel Gregg, Acton Institute

Advisory Board

Michael Novak, American Enterprise Institute, United States
Edward Younkins, Wheeling Jesuit University, United States
Manfred Spieker, University of Osnabrück, Germany
Jean-Yves Naudet, University of Aix-Marseilles, France
Maximilian Torres, University of Navarre, Spain
Rodger Charles, S.J., University of Oxford, England
Doug Bandow, Cato Institute, United States
Leonard Liggio, George Mason University, United States

Economics as a discipline cannot be detached from a historical background that was, it is increasingly recognized, religious in nature. Adam Ferguson and Adam Smith drew on the work of sixteenth- and seventeenth-century Spanish theologians, who strove to understand the process of exchange and trade in order to better address the moral dilemmas they saw arising from the spread of commerce in the New World. After a long period in which economics became detached from theology and ethics, many economists and theologians now see the benefit of studying economic realities in their full cultural, often religious, context. This new series, Studies in Ethics and Economics, provides an international forum for exploring the difficult theological and economic questions that arise in the pursuit of this objective.

Titles in the Series

Intelligence as a Principle of Public Economy / Del pensiero come principio d'economia publica, by Carlo Cattaneo
And Why Not? Morality and Business, by François Michelin
Faith and Liberty: The Economic Thought of the Late Scholastics, by Alejandro A. Chafuen
The Boundaries of Technique: Ordering Positive and Normative Concerns in Economic Research, by Andrew Yuengert

The Boundaries
of Technique

Ordering Positive and Normative Concerns in Economic Research

Andrew Yuengert

LEXINGTON BOOKS
Lanham • Boulder • New York • Toronto • Oxford

LEXINGTON BOOKS

Published in the United States of America
by Lexington Books
An imprint of The Rowman & Littlefield Publishing Group, Inc.
4501 Forbes Boulevard, Suite 200, Lanham, Maryland 20706

PO Box 317
Oxford
OX2 9RU, UK

British Library Cataloguing in Publication Information Available

Library of Congress Cataloging-in-Publication Data
Yuengert, Andrew, 1960–
   The boundaries of technique : ordering positive and normative concerns in
economic research / Andrew Yuengert.
      p. cm. — (Studies in ethics and economics)
   Includes bibliographical references and index.
   ISBN 0-7391-0706-2 (cloth : alk. paper) — ISBN 0-7391-0707-0 (pbk. : alk.
paper)
      1. Economics—Moral and ethical aspects. 2. Economics—Philosophy.
   3. Economics—Research. I. Title. II. Series.

   HB72.Y84 2004
   174—dc22   2003024405

Printed in the United States of America

∞ ™ The paper used in this publication meets the minimum requirements of
American National Standard for Information Sciences—Permanence of Paper
for Printed Library Materials, ANSI/NISO Z39.48-1992.

To Louis and Regina Yuengert

Piety is no substitute for technique.
—Etienne Gilson

Contents

Foreword

For too long social scientists, and particularly economists, have been confused on the distinction between positive economics and normative economics. They have tended to conflate useful methodological warnings with philosophical distinctions along the lines of the fact-value distinction.

Andrew Yuengert's book is a serious attempt to challenge these confusions by using categories such as prudence, judgment, and technique from an Aristotelian-Thomist point of view. He bends over backwards in giving both ethics and economics their due. He has personally struggled with reconciling his professional training (model-building and mathematics) with the good for human beings. He does not wish to surrender either. He is not willing to become a bad economist in order to be a good person.

It is, therefore, useful and constructive for economists to recognize the difference between "is" statements and "ought" statements. It is not useful and constructive to assume that all "ought" statements are subjective preferences and have no objective validity.

As an attempt to forestall premature moralizing, the positive-normative distinction between "what is" and "what ought to be" is a good guide for budding social scientists. H. L. Mencken said it all pretty pungently in his definition of an idealist: "An idealist is one who on noticing that a rose smells better than a cabbage also concludes that it will make better soup." In other words, a minimum wage of $50 an hour certainly sounds good and noble, but if you look at economic reality, what "is," you find that it will not work out as intended.

But there is a slippery slope from the positive-normative distinction to the fact-value distinction. A good analogy for the fact-value distinction is the alleged "wall of separation" between church and state in Supreme Court jurisprudence. Here there is also an attempted ironclad separation between two spheres—the religious, which is purely private, and the public, which is purely secular. The zealous attempt of the American Civil Liberties Union (ACLU) is to maintain an absolute fixed gulf between the two. If you violate this gulf, in the eyes of civil libertarians, you might as well go back to the witch burning and Inquisitions of old.

Most honest observers know the shaky foundations of this wall. The phrase "wall of separation" does not occur in the First Amendment, which only forbids Congress from establishing a religion; the phrase "wall of separation" only occurs in a private letter of Thomas Jefferson to a group of Baptists; the strict ACLU separation is violated all the time by Congress, the Supreme Court itself, the currency, and many state and local governments. None of these considerations have stopped the Supreme Court from incorporating the wall into its jurisprudence.

Then why should it be a fruitful analogy? Economists, by equating the positive-normative distinction with the fact-value distinction, create a dichotomy similar to the wall of separation by the ACLU. The analogy is suggestive because many who use the fact-value distinction are attempting to preserve a *purely private* understanding of the individual and the good society. The fact-value distinction does for ethics what the wall of separation does for religion: it purely privatizes it.

Many classical liberal and libertarian economists enshrine this in their understanding of the concept of individual liberty and/or Pareto optimality. The only changes that can be made are those to which people privately consent. The individual will is the trump card.

Even for those nonclassical liberals who create social welfare functions, the arbitrary nature of the public good is preserved because the constraints imposed—to achieve equality, for example—are considered to be the purely arbitrary will of the person creating the function. In other words, there can be no objective or rational discussion of the ethical ends because they are ultimately arbitrary.

Now how does Yuengert propose to get around these problems? To preserve the good of positive economics and the tools that economists have to learn in graduate school, he introduces the Aristotelian concept of *technique*. There are certain aspects of economics that correspond to Aristotelian technique, which is the process of making.

Technique has to be governed by prudence or you end up with the "efficient" killing machines of modern gangster movies or the modern spate of professional assassin movies like Robert Duvall's seductive *Assassination Tango* or John Cusack's humorous portrayal of Martin Blank in *Grosse Pointe Blank*.

I believe it was Irving Babbitt who said, "One must be a man before being an entomologist." Yuengert reminds us that it is incumbent on all economists, because they are human, to reflect on the hierarchy of ends. The economist is responsible for considering the ultimate ends of human action and ordering his activities accordingly.

The spirit of prudence to which Yuengert appeals is similar to that found in the 1789 preface to the Episcopalian *Book of Common Prayer*: "Seeking to keep the happy mean between too much stiffness in refusing, and too much easiness in admitting variations in things once advisedly established, she hath . . . yielded to make such alterations in some particulars, as in their respective times were thought convenient; yet so as that the main body and essential parts . . . have still been continued firm and unshaken."

The language of the "essential parts" can be contrasted to the "indifferent things." There are many things about which reasonable people can disagree. These are matters of subjective taste and preferences about which people do not have to see eye-to-eye. These are the realms of the *adiaphora*, the indifferent things. The economists, like the Stoics who originally developed the concept (but for different reasons), wished to dump all things into the category of *adiaphora* so that there would no longer be religious battles and controversies which had caused so much mischief in the wars of religion.

But prudence is preoccupied with the particularizing of situations that require judgment. Perhaps Yuengert should have added *casuistry*, a concept that has about as much appeal as castor oil to the modern mind, but which is far more salutary. *Casuistry* is simply the application of general principles to particular situations.

Prudence "governs the pursuit of human flourishing" and plays a larger role than the "prudence" of Adam Smith. Prudence in Adam Smith is very similar to "self-interest properly understood." It is concerned with pursuing real goods for oneself, for one's family, and for one's immediate community. Even this prudence is more focused than the tautological use of self-interest of most modern economists.

There is so much confusion between the categories of self-interest, selfishness, egoism, and utility maximization that several books need to be written on the subject. Yuengert is properly worried about the mind-set that economists receive in their training. Even those professors who work very hard to establish the fact that "utility maximization" does not really have a selfish content are usually unsuccessful. At the end of the course, students still seem to think that we are advocating or condoning selfishness and greed. Yuengert points to several studies which indicate that it is possible that this has an influence on the character of budding economists.

In many ways Yuengert's wrestling with these issues reminds me of the work of Wilhelm Roepke. Roepke attempted to liberate the positive-normative distinction from being shackled to the fact-value distinction coming down from the positivism of Max Weber. It is very unfortunate that a piece by Wilhelm Roepke, "A Value Judgment on Value Judgments," did not appear in the *American Economic Review* as it was supposed to, but only appeared in an obscure Turkish economic journal in 1942.

The Austrian tradition of Mises and Hayek was the basis for Roepke's work and methodology. Roepke would credit Mises with being more humane and nonscientistic than the neoclassical model builders. At the same time, Mises uses the "science of human action" in a way that does not conform to the Thomist tradition outlined by Yuengert. Mises would still proclaim the positive-normative distinction in ways that sound like the fact-value distinction.

The heady battles in German and Austrian circles inspired similar attacks on the fact-value distinction in political science. The critiques of Max Weber coming from Leo Strauss and Eric Voegelin attack the same relativism that vexes Roepke and Yuengert.

Yuengert's book goes a long way toward opening up these crucial fundamental questions and stopping the slippery slope from the positive-normative distinction to the fact-value distinction. We look forward to his next book in which he applies prudence and judgment to the policy questions that continue to vex us.

William F. Campbell
Emeritus Professor of Economics
Louisiana State University

Preface

This book is personal, of course—it is the culmination of my own struggle to come to grips with the role of ethics in my life as an economist. My interest in this topic was sparked early in my undergraduate career. Like most future PhDs, I fell in love with economics upon first contact. Economics appeared to make clear what had seemed mysterious before—the movements of interest rates, the arguments for free markets, the justifications for and arguments against government intervention in economic affairs.

At the time of my undergraduate studies, in the early 1980s, the U.S. Catholic bishops were deliberating about a teaching document on the U.S. economy, which eventually became *Economic Justice for All* (National Conference of Catholic Bishops 1986). These two developments—the bishops' writings and my undergraduate studies—together intrigued and challenged me. Both appeared true on their own terms, but in many ways what I was learning about markets seemed to be contradicted by the bishops' criticisms. This seeming conflict between two sources that I respected fueled my determination to get a PhD in economics, and then to explore the relationship between ethics and economics in my research.

Five years later I completed my PhD, but faced a disconcerting problem—I had been so well trained in the science of economics that I could no longer perceive any relationship between ethical reflection and economics. The irony of my predicament was not lost on me. I had been taught that economics had no ethical content, that it concerned itself solely with "what is"—observed behavior, the properties of certain mathematical models—and not with "what should be." I had not lost my conviction that ethical reflection had an important bearing on the conduct of my discipline, but I had been stripped of the intellectual tools necessary to discern the connections, and to reconcile ethics and economics. I was in an intellectual bind.

I have spent much of my academic career attempting to recover an account of the role of ethics in my discipline. In my reading I have glimpsed pieces of the account. These pieces are often seemingly contradictory. On the one hand, the postmodern critique appears to rule out any separation of economics from ethics, but it nevertheless seems to be true as far as it goes. On the other hand, positivist defenses of the autonomy of economics (as well as more recent, pragmatic defenses) also appear to be on to something true, as far as they go. The challenge has been to find out how far each of the accounts of ethics and economics actually goes, and to reconcile them.

I believe that an account of economics and ethics that begins with the rational agency of the economic researcher can reconcile both defenses of and attacks on value-free economics. Economics is not simply a set of sterile, ethically neutral propositions. It is a human endeavor to understand the economy and formulate advice about it. Even those who stress the understanding over the advising cannot deny that economists are purposive, even when their purpose is simply "to know." When the goal-oriented nature of economics is admitted, its ethical nature becomes undeniable.

This book offers an account of economics as a purposive—that is, human—enterprise. It draws on the thorough account of human action in the works of Saint Thomas Aquinas and Aristotle. The two philosophers do not have identical moral philosophies, but I draw mostly on those parts that are common to both—the formal account of human action, the role of reason in human action, and the place of technique in the moral life. I call the account "Thomistic," not to pick arguments with Aristotelians, but because Saint Thomas lived later, and "Aristotelian-Thomistic" takes too much space and sounds awkward.

Within the framework of this action-oriented moral philosophy, economics may still claim some autonomy from ethics, but only as a practical technique, and not as a logically separate category. The disciplinary boundary between ethics and economics makes sense only to the extent that it serves a human purpose—to the extent that it leads to a better understanding of the economy and promotes human development.

I could not have done this work without the support of Pepperdine University, which gave me a job despite my research interests in a field in which I was untrained; it has generously supported my efforts for nine years. Many friends and colleagues from the Association of Christian Economists and the Association for Social Economics have inspired and encouraged this work. I am grateful for words of encouragement at crucial junctures and very helpful comments from William Campbell, Chuck Wilber, Stephen Worland, Charles Clark, Andrew Foshee, Bruce Webb, and Colleen McCluskey. Father Al Barrera deserves special mention: his encyclopedic knowledge has been helpful at every turn, suggesting approaches and readings.

An early version of the argument in this book has been published previously as an article, "Why Did the Economist Cross the Road? The Hierarchical Logic of Ethical and Economic Reasoning," in *Economics and Philosophy* 18 (2002): 329–49. Parts of chapters 2 through 5 are reprinted with permission from that article.

Chapters 5 through 7 are a response to comments by a referee from the journal *Economics and Philosophy*, to the effect that markets for ideas are not purposive, and that therefore an agency-centered account of the discipline grants too great a role to economists' purposes and goals. His comment opened up a very fruitful avenue of inquiry for this book.

Serena Krombach, my editor at Lexington Books, patiently answered my questions about the details of preparing this manuscript for publication; her professional but friendly advice and encouragement were extremely helpful to a first-time book author. Sam Gregg, my series editor, was similarly encouraging about this project, and made a series of suggestions that have made the book more accessible to readers who are not economists.

My father-in-law, the late William Ryan, discerned a book in the articles I began writing on this topic several years ago. He read everything I have written, and offered both insight and encouragement to this project.

My wife, Elizabeth, made this book possible by her willingness nine years ago to move from comfortable New Jersey to the strange land of Southern California, far from home, friends, and family, in order to give me a chance to pursue this project, even though at the time it was not yet well-defined. I am grateful for her constant support, her demanding readings of the articles and manuscripts that led to this finished product, and her steady encouragement.

Andrew M. Yuengert
Malibu, California
May 2003

1

—ᴍ—

What Does Ethics Have to Do
with Economics?

When economists talk about positive and normative economics, they do not believe that the latter is *really* economics. Normative economics is actually applied ethics. Positive economics (*real* economics) is scientific, systematic inquiry into markets, prices, and other aspects of complex social interdependence. Normative economics makes use of the hard science of positive economics to inform choices that are inescapably moral. According to the conventions of mainstream economics, economists are engaged in economics only when they are investigating positive questions. It is part of the economist's creed that positive and normative analysis can be kept separate.

This book is about the positive-normative distinction; it is *not* about the fact-value distinction. The former distinction is a claim that economics and ethics are distinct human endeavors. Although the subject matter of economics is highly relevant to ethics, economics concerns itself with a set of narrower and more technical questions than ethics, and employs more formalized rules of practice. The latter distinction (first proposed by Scottish enlightenment philosopher David Hume 1955 [1740]) is a claim that prescriptive "ought" statements cannot be deduced from factual "is" statements. For example, facts such as "inflation lowers the income of the poor" do not by themselves justify the moral imperative "avoid inflation." Only the addition of a moral judgment, such as "one should avoid those things that lower the incomes of the poor" can give a fact moral force.[1]

1

It may seem strange that I begin by disavowing the fact-value distinction. To many economists, the positive-normative distinction *is* the fact-value distinction applied to economics. Most economics textbooks use the language of the fact-value distinction to describe the positive-normative distinction. For example, N. Gregory Mankiw's popular *Principles of Microeconomics* describes the positive-normative distinction thus: "*Positive statements* are descriptive. They make a claim about how the world *is*. . . . *Normative statements* are prescriptive. They make a claim about how the world *ought to be*" (p. 26).[2] The two distinctions are closely identified in the minds of economists.

The positive-normative distinction is not simply a special case of the fact-value distinction, however. The reality that the positive-normative distinction describes—the real (but not unlimited) autonomy of economics from ethics—is not fully captured by the logical categories "fact" and "value." The positive-normative distinction is broader and more complex; as we shall see, in the past it has been justified in terms of the division of labor, as a disciplinary space within which specialized technical expertise can produce greater understanding, as an encouragement for objectivity among researchers, and as a caution to be humble about the limited implications of research based on restrictive assumptions.

Because the two distinctions are conflated in the minds of most economists, it is not surprising that most recent attacks on the positive-normative distinction are actually narrow attacks on the fact-value distinction—even critics of the positive-normative distinction identify it with the fact-value distinction. Most philosophers of science reject any airtight distinction between facts and values—facts do not exist independent of the values of those who classify them as facts. Even if recent critiques of the fact-value distinction have merit, they do not constitute a conclusive repudiation of the positive-normative distinction, which describes a more complicated disciplinary reality.

Recent criticisms of the fact-value distinction give us an opportunity to disentangle the two distinctions, and to put the positive-normative distinction on a firmer footing: one that is less reliant on sharp lines of analytical demarcation, and more dependent on the professional judgment of economists; one that accepts the existence of economic technique, but which recognizes that it should emerge from, and be integrated into, the life project of the economist.

In this book I offer the moral philosophy of the medieval philosopher Thomas Aquinas as a firmer foundation for the positive-normative distinction. This chapter will outline the argument of the book. Before turning to that outline, we must first document how the positive-normative distinction became wedded to the fact-value distinction over the last one hundred years, and argue for a different approach.

For more than 160 years, dating back to Nassau Senior (1938 [1838]), the first chair in Political Economy at Oxford, economists have insisted that the subject matter and method of economics were to a significant degree insulated from ethical deliberations.[3] These early arguments were not based on the distinction between fact and value, between "what is" and "what ought to be." The most common early argument (Senior 1938 [1838] and Jevons 1878) relied on the division of labor: by specializing in the study of wealth creation, economics would produce more useful insights than if it became embroiled in broader, ethical debates. Many early arguments alluded to a broader field, separate from and above economics, called "legislation" by Adam Smith (1982 [1776]) and Senior (1938 [1838]) or "social philosophy" by the eighteenth-century utilitarian John Stuart Mill (1965 [1848]) and economist John Neville Keynes (1965 [1890]). This broader field drew on many subordinate fields to determine policy; its practice required prudential judgment in addition to purely technical expertise.

As the nineteenth century turned into the twentieth, arguments for a positive-normative distinction came to rely more heavily on the fact-value distinction. Although later writings by John Stuart Mill painted a more nuanced view of the ethics-economics divide, his early writings (Mill 1974 [1843]) assign to economics the formulation of "is" statements, and to social philosophy the formulation of "ought" statements. J. N. Keynes (1965 [1890]), whose work laid the groundwork for the modern positive-normative distinction, argued that economists are concerned with "theorems of fact, not practical precepts" (p. 13), echoing the categories of the fact-value distinction.[4]

With the rise of positivism in the twentieth century, the positive-normative distinction took its most extreme form. Positivism was a philosophy of science that denied the reality of anything that could not be measured and formally modeled. Science was the measure of all reality, and science required measurement. Added to this was a conviction that only hypotheses that could be tested against "facts" could be scientific. Along with positivism came the fact-value distinction as a guarantor of scientific objectivity: economics is about "what is," and ethics is about "what ought to be."

The economics profession embraced positivism in an attempt to put the discipline on a firm scientific footing. The rapid conversion to positivism began with the influential essay of English economist Lionel Robbins (1952 [1932]), and culminated in the classic defense of positivism in Milton Friedman (1953). Robbins placed the deliberations of economics and those of ethics in separate universes: "Between the generalizations of positive and normative studies there is a logical gulf fixed which no ingenuity can disguise and no juxtaposition in space or time bridge over. . . . Propositions involving the word 'ought' are different in kind from propositions involving the verb 'is'" (pp. 148–49).

The gulf between these two modes of discourse is unbridgeable. Further widening the ethics-economics gulf was the addition to the argument of an emotivist theory of ethics, which claimed that ethics was purely a matter of private tastes—tastes that could not be debated reasonably. Robbins stated this emotivist theory in the strongest possible terms: "If we disagree about ends, it is a case of thy blood or mine—or live and let live, according to the importance of the difference or the relative strength of our opponents" (p. 150). If emotivist claims are true, then economics and ethics become even more alien to one another. Not only are statements of economic fact logically disconnected from ethics: economic statements are amenable to reasoned analysis, and ethical statements are not. There is simply nothing for economists to talk about in ethics.[5]

Friedman (1953) restates Robbins's argument, but widens the gulf still further by claiming that most disagreements in economics can be resolved by positive economics:

> I venture the judgment, however, that . . . differences about economic policy among disinterested citizens derive predominantly from different predictions about the economic consequences of taking action—differences that in principle can be eliminated by the progress of positive economics—rather than from fundamental differences in basic values, differences about which men can ultimately only fight (p. 5).

According to Friedman, arguments over normative economics are not only unscientific; they are also unnecessary. Friedman's essay was enormously influential, and was the only methodological work read by at least two generations of economics graduate students.

By the late twentieth century, the positive-normative and fact-value distinctions were so closely identified as to be indistinguishable. Polish economist Kurt Klappholz (1984 [1964]) states and defends the mainstream positive-normative distinction entirely in the terms of the fact-value distinction, and Mark Blaug (1992), in what became the standard text on economic method, begins his discussion of the positive-normative distinction with the fact-value distinction, although he goes on to argue for a more empiricist, Popperian distinction.

Given the close identification of the two distinctions, it is no surprise that twentieth-century critics of the positive-normative distinction focused their attention on the fact-value distinction. Swedish Nobel Prize–winner Gunnar Myrdal (1984 [1954]) and I. M. Little (1950) both point out the implicit values in seemingly value-neutral "facts" like "national income" and "equilibrium." Historian of economic thought Robert Heilbroner (1973, 1990) and Charles Wilber and Roland Hoksbergen (1986) emphasize the role of ideological motivation in the formulation and practice of seemingly "positive" social science. Subroto Roy (1988) is more directly critical of the acceptance of emotivism in economics. Recently, critics have taken a postmodern turn, seeking to demonstrate the importance of rhetoric in economic discourse, and unmasking the interests that shape economic rhetoric (McCloskey 1994; Klamer, McCloskey, and Solow 1988; Mirowski 1991; Ferber and Nelson 1993).

In spite of the extensive criticism of the positive-normative distinction and its fact-value foundation, the distinction nevertheless persists in the minds of most economists. Nearly all undergraduate texts take the existence of a defensible boundary between positive and normative analysis for granted. Most practicing economists still describe their work in purely positive terms—that is, as analysis whose canons of technical practice (e.g., efficiency, consistency in estimation, parsimony) need not be revised with changes in the values which give rise to the questions investigated. Accordingly, they are puzzled at the implication that they should become students of moral philosophy, or worse yet, students of morals—or even worse yet, students of French philosophy.

Of course, this state of affairs may be due to a stubborn refusal on the part of most economists to accept that their discipline is ethics-laden. This cannot be the full story, however. The continued popularity of the positive-normative distinction must be due in part to its continued *plausibility*, even after its fact-value foundations are knocked out from under it. After all, the positive-normative distinction seemed credible enough to early economists like Adam Smith, Nassau Senior, and even John Stuart Mill (on his better days); none of these relied entirely on the fact-value distinction to justify the positive-normative distinction.

The fact-value distinction is of course relevant to the positive-normative distinction, but the two distinctions are not identical. The positive-normative distinction is more complex and richer than the fact-value distinction; it deserves a better, more complex defense. The fact-value distinction is in some ways a distraction: the sharp divisions it claims, and the vigorous debates over those divisions, obscure the more subtle distinction between the deliberations of ethics and the deliberations of economics.

The battles over the fact-value distinction have served a useful purpose in revealing that the sharp distinctions between different kinds of human inquiry (scientific versus ethical, religious versus political, for example) cannot be as airtight as the modern world would like them to be. Because of this debate, it has become evident that the claim that economics is "value-free" in every possible sense of the term is untenable. This sweeping claim was made by neither Robbins (1952 [1932]) nor Friedman (1953), although Friedman came close in his assertion that most disagreements were resolvable by positive economics. The other extreme—that every conceivable statement an economist makes is fully determined by his value judgments—is equally implausible. Surely there can be disinterested differences of opinion about technique and fact, and these differences can affect the content of economic analysis independently of the influence of value judgments (Klappholz 1984 [1964]). Clearly, the question is not "Is economics completely separate from ethics?" This all-or-nothing question has its roots in the purely logical distinctions between fact and value. Instead, the question is "In what sense, if any, is economics separated from ethics, and in what sense, if any, is economics affected by ethical considerations?" As Mark Blaug (1992) notes, "There is clearly much sorting out to be done here" (p. 112).

Because direct attacks on the fact-value distinction are only oblique attacks on the positive-normative distinction, they often leave economists puzzled. Defenders of the positive-normative distinction are left with the impression that its critics are attacking the wrong distinction, one that is much too sweeping, and more ambitious than that claimed by J. N. Keynes or Robbins. According to this line of defense, because the distinction that is under attack is a straw man, the attacks on it are trivially true, but irrelevant. For example, Klappholz (1984 [1964]) is not swayed by claims that there are no value-free facts; instead, he maintains that the descriptive statements of economics, however value-laden, cannot be used to infer normative conclusions. Criticisms of the positive-normative distinction that draw attention to the role of values in motivating the choice of topic and the formulation of concepts do not affect the "logical neutrality of economics" (p. 279). However biased the concepts themselves, their use in description does not of itself justify any policy conclusion.[6] In making this point, Klappholz restates the analysis of the pioneer sociologist Max Weber (1949), who asserted the possibility of objectivity at the same time he acknowledged the inevitable role of values in the choice of research topics and the formulation of theoretical concepts.[7]

Mark Blaug (1992), in defending the positive-normative distinction, is less concerned about saving the fact-value distinction, and more anxious to defend Popperian research norms, which accept as scientific only those statements that are falsifiable.[8] According to Blaug, attacks on the fact-value distinction do not endanger the positive-normative distinction. The latter is a distinction between statements which are in principle falsifiable—that is, Popperian—and those which are not falsifiable even in principle. Blaug asserts that what are often presented as examples of value-laden "positive" statements are not in fact "positive" statements, but are instead unexamined, untestable, unfalsifiable assumptions. The progress of economics will come only through arduous efforts to test theories against data.

Intriguingly, Blaug's attempt to distance the positive-normative distinction from the fact-value distinction goes beyond a restatement of Popperian falsifiability. It points the way toward a different sort of defense of an ethics-neutral space for economics—one that relies more on the shared standards of a community of scholars. He begins by accepting that fact and value statements are similar in one important respect: "The acceptance or rejection of is-statements is not a very different cognitive process from the acceptance or rejection of ought-statements; my contention is that there are no empirical, descriptive is-statements regarded as true that do not rely on a definite social consensus that we 'ought' to accept that is-statement" (p. 114).

According to Blaug, statements of positive economics are identified as such because a community of scholars agree to accept the standards (or values) which qualify them as positive economics. These standards are developed to resolve disagreements about statements of fact. As MIT economist Sidney Alexander (1967) notes, positive judgments, like normative judgments, are interpersonally valid only among those who share the same point of view.[9] The standards can be thought of as the outcome of a coordination game among economists (Klein 1999).

The standards that define positive economics are of course value-laden. They are shared by persons in the community of scholars that develop and teach them; schools of economists are *defined* by their shared values, and the standards which promote them. In mainstream economics, these standards include consistency in estimation, parsimony in modeling, falsifiability, openness to criticism, and honesty and openness in deriving, formulating, and reporting research results. The philosopher of science Michael Polanyi (1962) observes that belief always involves a commitment; more often than not, the beliefs of economists are embedded in a commitment to the shared values of a community of inquiry. Individuals and groups of economists do not always adhere to these standards in the breach, but most accept them as an ideal to which their critics may appeal. An economist may deny that his estimates are inconsistent, but he will not deny that consistency is desirable. He may not in fact be open to criticism, but he will accept that he should be.

The admission that economists operate in scholarly communities whose shared commitments to certain goods motivate and justify their canons of practice need not endanger the positive-normative distinction. Crucial to the maintenance of a separate sphere for ethics-neutral economics is that the values which inform positive economics are independent of what are sometimes called "ethical" values: policy concerns, religious precepts, and personal commitments. Hausman and McPherson (1996), developing the insights of Blaug, define a value-free sphere of inquiry where questions of fact are debated, and "in which the answers are not influenced by any values apart from those which are part of the science itself" (p. 212). This is a claim that economists who disagree on "ethical" goals like commitment to the poor can still agree on shared standards of economic inquiry—parsimony, a commitment to mathematical formalism, and so forth.

In Blaug's and Hausman and McPherson's framework, positive economics is defined not as a value-free sphere, but as a sphere whose values are *self-contained*. On a given research question, economists need not appeal to values outside of those embodied in economic method. Those procedures and techniques that do not change with the "outside" ethical values that direct them are called "positive economics." The argument over positive and normative then becomes a debate about which procedures are invariant, or should be invariant, to changes in the values that give rise to research questions.

The acknowledgment that the practice of positive economics is governed by values, however self-contained, moves the discussion away from the logical content of "is" and "ought" statements and toward the motivation and justification of those statements. It raises a new set of questions, and demands a fuller account of human motivation:

1. How do scholarly communities decide which self-contained values to adopt, and how do they form around those values?
2. In what sense are these values self-contained, insulated from values "outside" of the field?

In this book I will not address the first question directly, although the answers to it are relevant to our inquiry. The first question provides inspiration for the literature on the sociology of social science (Kuhn 1970, 1977; Lakatos 1978; Bernstein 1983; Hands 2001). The second question is the focus of this book. I will offer an integrated account of human values in economics that can accommodate both the "ethical" values from which economists wish to insulate themselves, and the "methodological" values which govern economics.

Economics does not have a very satisfying answer to the second question because it approaches the positive-normative distinction from the perspective of analytical philosophy. The analytic approaches that dominated twentieth-century defenses of positive social science were characterized by careful analysis of language and meaning. The positive-normative distinction, expressed in analytic terms, became a distinction between different kinds of statements: assertions of "fact" and assertions of "value." In line with Hume (1955 [1740]), statements of fact did not entail any statements of value, nor did they require any statements of value as premises. The two sorts of statement were entirely distinct.

Analytic approaches ask: Does a particular statement or argument in economics depend on or entail any value claims? Defenders of a stark separation of economics from ethics answer "no." The critics of the positive-normative split answer "yes," laying bare the value-content in statements of fact (Myrdal 1984 [1954]), or carefully analyzing the role of value-laden premises in seemingly purely scientific arguments (Hausman and McPherson 1996).

For all its valuable contributions, the analytical controversy over fact and value is only partially enlightening. Blaug (1992) and Hausman and McPherson (1996) accept the importance of the values of the community of economists, but do not give a systematic account of those values beyond their logical implications for positive economics. Weston (1994) gives a pragmatic defense of the positive-normative distinction that refers frequently to its role in safeguarding values internal to the practice of economics, but his account is equally unsystematic.

The exhaustive analytical treatment of fact and value is useful in that it helps economists to understand the role played by ethical precepts in their reasoning. It nevertheless fails to provide an account of why economists should make one sort of statement or another. Why should we be motivated to keep the two kinds of statements separate? If the positive-normative distinction is not airtight, should we strive to plug the leaks, or simply get used to a messier, value-impregnated methodology?

In other words, when addressing the role of ethics in economic analysis, the most important question on economists' minds is a practical one: What should we *do* differently? Does the controversy make a difference to our daily tasks as economists? If so, how? From the perspective of the analytical approach, the connections between fact and value, although accepted by philosophers, are obscured by a century of highly technical controversy (barely touched upon here), and are as a result difficult for economists untrained in philosophy to perceive or accept. Moreover, it is not clear how economists should act in response to the analytical critique.

It is the thesis of this book that an alternative account of the positive-normative distinction can be formulated from the moral philosophy of the medieval philosopher and theologian Thomas Aquinas. Thomas Aquinas's work combines the insights of Augustinian and Aristotelian philosophy, but the formal framework for his moral philosophy is Aristotelian. The Thomistic approach differs from recent analytical approaches in that its focus is on human action—it is practical, not theoretical. Such an account will focus on the values of economists (we will call them "ends") and the ways in which they are expressed in research actions.

Thomas Aquinas's moral theory is a careful, thorough account of human action. The advantage of examining economics from the perspective of the actions of economists is that human action is inescapably moral: the moral status of human action is accepted even by positivists. Since there

is less controversy over the connections between human action and ethical reflection, the Thomistic tradition offers an alternative from which to
view the relationship of ethics to economics—an alternative that is not en-
cumbered by modern disputes over facts and values.

The inherently moral character of human action is acknowledged by
both critics and advocates of distance between ethics and economics.
British economist John A. Hobson (1901) is critical of the analytical distinction between ethics and economics, and appeals to human action as a
grounds for a moral treatment of economics: "The verbal boundaries put
up by specialist treatises on ethics and politics are passed over on every
page wherever conduct is in question" (p. 62). More recently, the Aristotelian economist Ricardo Crespo (1998) grounds his argument that economics is a moral science in its analysis of human action: "When action is
viewed from the perspective of the agent, I think its moral nature is in-
controvertible" (p. 202). Neither is this insight lost on those who adopt the
analytical approach. Hausman and McPherson (1996), in an aside to their
thorough analytical treatment of the ethics-economics split, refer to the inherently moral nature of the conduct of economists: "To speak of a 'value-
free' inquiry may be misleading. It suggests that the *conduct* of the inquiry
is value-free. But the conduct of inquiry cannot possibly be value-free. Inquiring involves action, and action is motivated by values" (p. 212).

Thomistic analysis, because it takes as its subject human action and its
motivation, offers a framework within which to think about the positive-
normative distinction and its practical implications for what economists
do. The Thomistic framework does not focus on the morality of models or
estimation techniques—the morality of the abstraction *homo economicus*,
for example—since intellectual constructs are not in themselves good or
evil in the same way that human action is. Consequently, I will not take a
position on reality in mathematical modeling, or on the need to take institutions seriously; my critique is not of unreal models, but of the actions
of real economists. Neither will I analyze the morality of economic behavior, or the role of morality in the economy. The object of the analysis is
the behavior of economists going about the ordinary business of their
lives—theoretical and empirical research and application. This move—
from the analysis of abstract economic concepts to the analysis of the concrete research decisions of economists—allows us to focus more closely on
the justifications and motivations for "what economists do."

A focus on human behavior and its motivation does not exclude from
consideration the desirability of various economic concepts. An economic
concept is only good or bad as it produces good or bad effects in action
when it is used by economists. For example, if *homo economicus* is a bad assumption, then it stands to reason that an economist should not employ
it. But what makes it a bad assumption? Only the context in which the de-

cision to employ the assumption is made: the desirability of the goals of the research, and the role of the assumption in advancing the research toward those goals. A concept is bad, or immoral, only to the extent that it fails to advance some worthy goal when it is used, or that it advances some undesirable goal. Thus, economists should not employ the assumption of *homo economicus* if its use fails to help them understand and predict market behavior and outcomes, or if its rhetorical use promotes a narrow selfishness that inhibits the development in students of otherwise natural commitments to the common good.[10]

We will explore Aquinas's account of human action only at its most general level. The analysis is purely formal: it does not depend on Aquinas's or Aristotle's arguments locating the good life in beatitude or virtue, but relies instead on Aquinas's exploration of the nature of practical reasoning—of how human beings attempt to achieve their ends through action. Thomistic analysis of the human act makes clear the ways in which we make "should" statements about economics—about the direction and content of economic research, and the advice economists give. As we shall see, a Thomistic framework cuts two ways. It rejects an economic science completely cut off from ethics; at the same time, it recognizes a limited (but by no means complete) autonomy of economic technique within ethical inquiry. Within the tradition there are warnings about the consequences of conducting economic analysis as if ethical concerns were irrelevant.

Chapter 2 is an introduction to Aquinas's moral philosophy. Human beings, endowed with will and reason, are able to deliberate about the good, and act to achieve it. Human action, according to Aquinas, is *defined* as action that is reasoned and purposeful, characterized by deliberation about the ends (or goals) of human life and the means for achieving those ends. Action that is not directed to an end is not intelligible, cannot be reasoned about. Human beings do not always act reasonably, but reasoned reflection on what it means to live a good human life, and on the means to achieve it, is supposed to improve the prospects of actually achieving human happiness. Because it reasons from human purposes, Thomistic philosophy is teleological ("telos" means purpose or function).

The Thomistic account of human action is at the same time an account of rationality and an account of morality—reason and morals are closely connected. When humans reason about their actions, they refer their actions to ends. These ends have an undeniable moral force: our actions are both justified and motivated by ends. This connection between rationality and ethics should be intriguing to economists, who make assumptions of rationality the centerpiece of theory, but are uncomfortable with moral claims.

Chapter 2 concludes with a reflection on rationality and morality, and what the connection between the two implies for economic practice.

Economists work with a relatively thin, instrumental form of rationality, whose focus is on the efficient accomplishment of fixed, well-specified goals. In contrast, Thomistic rationality is broader; it incorporates deliberation about ends as well as means, and the ends it posits are less quantifiable than those of economics. Because rationality and morality are connected (a certain rationality implies a corresponding morality and vice versa), this more complex rationality is a significant barrier to the translation of Thomistic insights into economic language. Economists will need to expand their notion of rationality in order to understand Aquinas's insights into the moral nature of human activity, including their own activity as economists.

Chapter 3 explores the order among the ends of human action. Human beings act for multiple ends. Some ends are proximate, subordinate to other ends, and desirable only insofar as they promote those further ends. Some ends are ultimate, that is, intrinsically desirable. This order among ends is complex, but is inherent in the exercise of practical reason. Fully intelligible human action must be for intrinsically valuable ends. For the most part, the ends toward which economists labor as economists are proximate. For example, correct inferences from formalized statistical or other mathematical models are necessary to inform and develop policy in pursuit of ethical ends: efficiency, welfare, poverty relief, and so forth.

Chapter 4 uses the framework of chapters 2 and 3 to outline the relationship between the proximate ends of economics and the higher-order ends to which they are subordinate. Three principles govern the relationship. The first is the priority of higher-order ends over economics, which rules out a complete separation of economics from ethics. The ends of economics are proximate, and as such economic research can only be motivated by ultimate ends. These ultimate ends may be mundane (fame, a good living for the economist and his or her family) or lofty (knowledge, the elimination of poverty); whatever they are, economists act to promote them through the proximate ends of their research. Without ultimate ends, there is no reason to be an economic researcher: economics is *for* ethics. Moreover, one size proximate end does not fit all ultimate ends: concepts, measurements, and modeling strategies should be tailored to best promote the ultimate ends of the researcher.

Thomistic analysis integrates the practice of economics into the moral life of the researcher, and thus rejects the existence of a sanitized, value-free analysis, if by "analysis" one means "the actions of researchers," and not simply "a set of logically related claims and assertions." In spite of this rejection of a complete separation of economics from ethics, the second and third principles provide space for a self-contained, "positive" economics, although in place of the word "positive" Aquinas would have used the word "technical."

The second principle asserts the limited neutrality of techniques. In Aquinas, a positive-normative distinction emerges, not from any separation of fact from value, but from a distinction between types of reason. The types of reason most directly relevant to our inquiry are "prudence" and "technique." Prudence governs the pursuit of human flourishing, and as such governs all of man's activities. Its domain is ethical deliberation. Technique governs the production of things external to man—material things like chairs, and immaterial things like regressions and economic models. An activity qualifies as a technique to the extent that it has been systematized. Through extensive reflection on the experience of making, a technique develops its own canons of practice. The exercise of technique does not require prudential judgment, and goodness in a technique is somewhat separate from goodness in general. We may call someone "technically good" without implying that he is a "good person."

The Thomistic category "technique" offers a promising avenue by which to understand both the ways in which ethics affects economics and the ways in which it should not. Consequently, it offers a framework within which to accomplish the integration of technical and ethical approaches to economics called for by Nobel Prize–winning economic philosopher Amartya Sen (1987). Sen describes two traditions of economics: an "ethics-related" tradition, going back to Aristotle (1941a, 1941b), and the "engineering" approach, which is more concerned with "primarily logistic issues rather than with ultimate ends" (p. 4). Sen claims that the ethics approach has been ignored, and that economics as a result has been impoverished. He argues for a combination of the two approaches: "I would like to argue that the deep questions raised by the ethics-related view of motivation and of social achievement must find an important place in modern economics, but at the same time it is impossible to deny that the engineering approach has much to offer economics as well" (p. 6).

What Sen calls the "engineering" approach sounds a lot like "technique" in the Aristotelian and Thomistic sense. The "ethics-related" view therefore has already created the categories necessary to combine Sen's two approaches. The analysis will have to be developed to address the challenges raised by modern approaches to technique, however.

Economists need not appeal to Aristotelian technique to justify some ethics-neutral space for their discipline. A third principle, the inviolability of truth, can also provide justification. The presence of an ultimate end—knowledge—within the purview of economics grants even technical economic practice a certain moral weight. Knowledge, though of course useful in the pursuit of other goals, is also good in itself. The Thomistic tradition demands special treatment for ultimate goods—they may not be treated as purely instrumental. One cannot compromise the truth, even in service of desirable ends.

The introductory analysis and application of chapters 2, 3, and 4 is enough to lay out the basic framework of the Thomistic approach, but its full application requires a careful discussion of the differences between the social context in which Aquinas wrote and the modern context. Chapter 5 is devoted to this discussion.

Needless to say, Aquinas wrote for an audience whose intellectual formation and presuppositions were different from our own in important ways. Aquinas's thirteenth-century theology students (and Aristotle's aristocratic students seventeen centuries before) would have been very comfortable with the close connections between the proximate ends of their actions and the ultimate ends pursued in society. Society itself was organized explicitly around the pursuit of ultimate ends, whether they be the ends of the polis in Athens or the ends of Christendom in Europe. In contrast, the modern metaphor for human activity, be it intellectual or material, is market exchange. The marketplace is not an acting agent and is not explicitly committed to or directed to any particular end. Individuals in markets are assumed to pursue ends which are very close to their personal material interests; in the course of this pursuit individuals sometimes promote the self-interested goals of others in return for help in advancing their own. There are important outcomes of this process of exchange that are not intended by any participant. Indeed, the unintended outcomes of market exchange may be more desirable than outcomes that result from intentional manipulations of the system. It is not clear that the Thomistic analysis of goal-oriented agency has any purchase on a moral environment so full of contingency and unintended consequences.

This argument is likely to be persuasive to many economists, schooled as they are in the invisible hand. Chapter 5 explores how market interactions affect the ordered chain of ends that motivate and justify human action, and which undergird Thomistic moral theory. Exchange does not negate the Thomistic insights, but it does add a layer of complexity to the Thomistic account of human action that enriches it in two ways.

First, it complicates the ordered chain of ends, by incorporating into it the ends of others—ends that the acting individual has agreed to promote in exchange. It does not, however, sever the connection between ultimate and proximate ends. For example, if you are a paid consultant advising an agency that is promoting development in a rural area, it matters not whether you are helping them in order to make a living, or whether you would work for free. In either case, development as an end should motivate and guide the analysis that shapes your advice.

Second, the market account puts a greater distance between the goals of policy and the ends of researchers, since economists may pursue certain ends in research only to make a living or to get tenure, and as a result may care little about the goals that motivate researchers to pay them. The purchasers of economic research (granting agencies and governments) may find themselves as principal in a principal-agent problem, unable to control self-serving behavior on the part of their agents, the economists.[11] This market approach makes the modern separation of technique and ultimate ends clear in a way that may be missed in the Thomistic framework.

From the perspective of this market account, the Thomistic framework seems to lend credence to the positivist Robbinsian story of the technical economist who pursues ends specified by a policymaker; researchers need not involve themselves in deliberations about the policy ends of their employers. The Thomistic response to this cannot be taken without modification from Aquinas, since he did not anticipate the sharp modern separation of technique from the pursuit of ultimate goals, and formulated no response to it beyond the claim that such a pursuit was unintelligible. Nevertheless, a response to the modern exchange-based separation of technique from ethics can be composed from modern critics of that separation.

Chapter 6 critiques the isolation of technique from prudence in the modern context. First, the moral evaluation of a technique can never be completely separated from the evaluation of the ends that it serves. Even hireling economists bear, and often acknowledge, some moral responsibility for the uses to which their analysis is put by others. Second, philosophers as diverse as John Cardinal Newman (1982 [1852]), Benedetto Croce (1913), and Joseph Dunne (1993) caution that technique isolated from prudence tends to exalt its proximate ends as ultimate, to the detriment of the overall human good. This substitution of the ends of technique for human ends is a recurring theme of modernity.

Chapter 6 accepts the claim that economics is a technique, and cautions against the exercise of that technique in moral isolation. In contrast, chapter 7 examines economics' claim to be a technique. It begins with a comparison of technique and prudence. Technique produces results that are external to the technician, and is carried out according to a well-developed body of knowledge about making; prudence (which governs all human action) results in the internal development of the human who acts prudently, and is learned through experience, in the company of those who are prudent. Economic analysis may not meet this strict definition of technique, and may instead be closer to prudence, whose practice must engage ultimate ends more directly. For example, training in economics develops the intellectual habits and identity of the student; the result of the training is a not simply a person who possesses certain intellectual tools, but a person who has "become an economist." Moreover, when economics is applied to a new area, where its ends are not clearly specified, it becomes less a technique and more a species of prudence. This last point will bring us back to the contrast between the narrow, instrumental rationality of economics, and the more complex rationality of Aquinas and the Thomistic tradition.

Chapter 8 summarizes the book, and advises economists to reflect upon the motivation and justification for their work. I will also point out the continuities between the Thomistic approach outlined here and recent analytical research on the positive-normative distinction. The insights of the book, if taken to heart, need not result in a radical revision of research programs, but they may make researchers more comfortable talking about values in economics.

It is not scandalous that values influence the research decisions of economists. From the Thomistic perspective, this influence is not an embarrassing mistake, to be corrected by a renewed commitment to positivist orthodoxy. Rather, it is a natural consequence of the fact that economists are human. These values should be openly acknowledged and discussed, in order to make economics more fruitful. Every economist should take the time to investigate and question the chain of ends that motivate his or her research. Even the most cursory examination of the full chain of human ends served by a research project may result in research questions and procedures that promote more efficiently the ends of the researcher. If the higher-order ends of a given research project are taken without reflection from the field or popular culture, then economists will advance the goals they actually care about only accidentally.

NOTES

1. The deduction of an "ought" statement solely from "is" statements is often called the "naturalistic fallacy."

2. Mankiw (1998).

3. For a history of the separation of economics from moral philosophy, see Drakopoulos (1991), Blaug (1992), Redman (1997), Vickers (1997), and Backhouse (2002, ch. 7).

4. Keynes proposes a three-part division of economics, adding to normative and positive economics a third category, the "art" of economics. The "art" of economics might be included in normative economics today, although Colander (1994) argues that it is a separate category of economic analysis.

5. Roy (1988) criticizes the popularity of emotivist theories in economics, as do McCloskey (1994) and Hausman and McPherson (1996). It is acknowledged to be an extreme view, unfortunately popular among economists, due to the influential essay by Friedman (1953). Machlup (1969) criticizes the characterization of value judgments as meaningless (on the same order as gibberish) as too harsh and sweeping. For a philosophical critique of emotivism, see MacIntyre (1984).

6. Machlup (1969) makes a similar point.

7. Machlup (1969) also appeals to Weber in response to Myrdal's argument that economic concepts were value-impregnated, claiming that Weber had put the issue to rest by establishing the possibility of objectivity even when one's concepts reflect one's values.

8. A falsifiable statement is one that can in principle be shown to be false through observation.

9. In principle, "ought" statements can also be resolved by appeal to shared standards of argument; unfortunately, such a shared body of standards has not existed since before the Enlightenment.

10. The argument that the employment of the assumption of *homo economicus* promotes a narrow selfishness in students is made in Alexander (1967), Etzioni (1988), and Radin (1996). Marwell and Ames (1981), Carter and Irons (1991), and Frank, Gilovich, and Regan (1993) provide empirical evidence for this claim.

11. A principal-agent problem involves someone who wants something done—a "principal"—and the person hired to do it—the "agent." The reason the principal hires the agent is that the agent has expertise and information about the task to be accomplished (the lawyer knows the law, the economist knows economic research) which the principal lacks. The problem is that the agent may take advantage of the principal's ignorance to promote his own interests at the expense of his boss, the principal. Economists may amuse themselves with mathematical games, for example, even though those games do not in fact promote understanding of the economy, and the noneconomist principals may not be expert enough to unmask the fraud.

2

—⁓—

Why Did the Economist Cross the Road? Morality and Rationality in Thomistic Moral Philosophy

Science has no goals. Only individuals have goals.

—Ronald Coase (1994a)

The old joke about why the chicken crossed the road is too familiar to be funny anymore, but it is worth asking why it ever was funny. It is funny because the punch line (to get to the other side) is unexpected; it is obviously true, but incomplete. We expect the punch line to tell us *why* the chicken wanted to get to the other side—in order to see a man lay bricks, for example. This answer is still incomplete, in much the same way as the first answer was; we might still ask why the chicken wants to see a man lay bricks. If the answer to this question is that the chicken has never seen a man lay a brick, we might ask again why the chicken should want to see something that it has not seen before. The answer to this next question may be "because variety is the spice of life." At this point, since the chicken appears to seek variety for its own sake, there are no further questions to be asked, unless we wish to dispute the desirability of variety.

Each of the answers given above, except perhaps the last, is incomplete in some way. If the chicken's behavior is rationally directed toward a set of ordered ends, then the full meaning of the action "cross the road" can only be discovered within this hierarchically ordered reason. Each answer reveals a goal or end, some of which are ultimate ends, but many of which are themselves subordinate means to some further end. The chicken would not cross the road if the bricklayer were not laying bricks on the other side; similarly, he would not watch the man lay bricks if he had seen such a thing many times before.

Chickens do not display human rationality, of course—the one in the joke may well be simply trying to get to the other side, without any further end in sight. The point of the joke, nevertheless, is that humans, being rational, look for a fully rational explanation. A chicken crossing the road without purpose may not be notable; a person who cannot give a full, hierarchical explanation of his own road crossing might reasonably be described as a chicken running around with his head cut off. Any explanation of human action that breaks off short of a more extensive account of the motivation of the acting human agent is incomplete and, we suspect, unexamined. Often this incompleteness is unobjectionable; we do not need to give a full accounting of the reasons for our actions when the full accounting is self-evident to those with whom we are conversing. Nonetheless, we expect human beings to evaluate their actions with their goals in mind.

This seeking for explanation and justification for action is quintessentially human. Our inquiring minds are seldom satisfied with incomplete accounts, such as "to get to the other side." What is true for human action in general is particularly true for scholarship, including economic research. Scholars, more than other humans, are supposed to subject everything they do to reasoned inquiry. When economists posit theories, specify models, collect data, and estimate empirical relationships, they are in pursuit of ordered goals. They often find themselves giving an account both of the desirability of the ends as well as the suitability of the means of their research. A labor economist runs a regression to discover the effects of job training programs on the subsequent employment of the trainee; he desires to discover the effect of job training in order to advise lawmakers on the desirability of public investment in job training programs; these programs, if effective, should be publicly funded in order to alleviate the hardships of inner city youth; and so on.

Economists sometimes give truncated justifications for their actions, such as "to generate consistent estimates," or "in order to derive a well-behaved utility function." If there is not some set of further, unspoken goals served by the technical actions of economists, then these accounts are not fully rational; they are equivalent to the punch line of the joke: "to get to the other side." Most of the time, economists implicitly acknowledge the need for a full account of their actions, even as they adopt the role of mere technical advisors. They may claim that the knowledge produced by their efforts is self-evidently good, and need not be justified by appeal to its promotion of some further end; more often, they justify the insights of their research by referring to the important policy implications of the analysis.[1]

This hierarchical account of human action is the basis for Thomistic moral philosophy. This chapter and the next are a brief introduction to the Thomistic framework. I will begin by pointing out the similarities between moral and technical prescription. Although economists reject moral prescriptions (e.g., feed the poor, avoid excessive income inequality) as irrelevant to their practice, and accept technical prescriptions (e.g., do not overly complicate your models) as fully constitutive of sound method, the two sorts of statements are actually quite similar. Their similarities highlight the connection between rationality and morality in Thomistic analysis. The Thomistic analysis of the human act makes clear the ways in which we make "should" statements as economists—about the direction and content of economic research, and the advice economists give. It also makes clear how prescriptive statements of any sort draw their moral force from rationality.

THE HUMAN ACT: RATIONALITY AND MORALITY

Choose instruments that are uncorrelated with the dependent variable.
Do not trade with a country which oppresses its own people.

To the modern scientific mind, these two prescriptive statements are of different types. The first belongs to the set of technical prescriptions; the second belongs to the set of moral prescriptions. There are defensible reasons for this division, as we shall see in chapter 4; nevertheless, the division should not blind us to the essential similarity of the two statements, and the two kinds of arguments.

The prescriptive force of each of the above statements can only be grasped by an understanding of the goals advanced by the prescription. By "goal" I mean "that which is thought to be good by the acting person"; in this book I will use the terms "goal," "end," and "good" interchangeably. Uncorrelated instruments are desirable because they advance the goal of consistent estimation; the refusal to trade with oppressive regimes is supposed to express a commitment to freedom, and to pressure an oppressive government to liberalize. In each case, the ends of the acting person (those pursued directly in the act as well as the person's other ends) provide the only context within which the prescriptive force of the statement can be understood, and either assented to or repudiated. Indeed, effective arguments against either of these statements must take one of three forms:

1. The proposed action does not in fact advance the implicit goal.
2. The implicit goal is not in fact good; its goodness is only apparent.
3. The proposed action is inimical to some other worthy goal, even if it advances the implicit goal.[2]

Viewed from this perspective, prescriptive statements about technical matters and prescriptive statements about moral matters are similar, and share the same logical structure: both advise the listener how to achieve a particular end. Although the ends of the technical statement (consistency) may be less controversial than the ends of the moral statement (do not abet oppression), both statements draw their moral force, their "ought-ness," from the desirability of the end in question and the efficiency with which the prescribed action achieves its end.

That any prescription for action toward ends is inherently moral is a point not lost on economic philosophers. In the last chapter, a sample of quotes (Hobson 1901, Crespo 1998, Hausman and McPherson 1996) attested to an awareness that the ethical nature of human action is incontestable. It is for this reason that a philosophical approach that focuses on the actions of economic researchers allows us to explore the nature of the relationships between ethics and economics without becoming embroiled in controversies over fact and value.

This basic structure of prescriptive reasoning (that it is oriented toward human ends) is the starting point for the moral philosophy of Aristotle and Thomas Aquinas. Both arrive at this account of moral reasoning in the course of reflection about what it means to reason well about action. In order to reason well about human action, it is necessary to understand what a human act is, and what it means to act humanly well. Before we can describe what it means to act humanly well, we must begin with an account of excellence, applied toward human acts.

I use the term "excellence" here instead of "goodness" to avoid confusing the desirability of an end (goodness) with quality of function (excellence). "Excellence" is synonymous with "virtue" in Aristotle and Aquinas. This definition of virtue is different from the common modern definition. Since Immanuel Kant (the eighteenth-century German rationalist philosopher), virtue has been defined as a commitment, expressed through the passions, to follow moral rules. This modern location of virtue in the passionate commitments of the person is evident in the work of modern social philosopher John Rawls, one of the few moral philosophers to whom economists pay attention. Rawls (1971) defines moral virtue as "strong and normally effective desires to act on the basic principles of right" (p. 436).[3] By this definition, a virtuous person is someone who has the strength of will to commit to a moral rule, whatever that rule happens to be. This definition of virtue must not be confused with Thomistic virtue, defined as "human excellence." Aristotle's and Aquinas's definitions of virtue are tied closely to their philosophical anthropology. Discussions of virtue cannot be separated from discussions about the nature and purpose of the human person.

In Aquinas, excellence, both in a narrow sense (an excellent flute player) and in a broader, moral sense (a virtuous person), is defined relative to function. For example, a watch is an excellent watch if it does what a watch should do, in the way that a watch should—if it mechanically keeps the time accurately, with a minimum of fuss. Similarly, a human being is excellent if he or she acts the way a human should to achieve the ends of human life.[4]

Within this framework, of course, the judgment of a person's moral excellence depends on the discernment of what is characteristically human. Again, the analogy of the watch helps to make this point. We may describe a particular watch as excellent because it keeps time well, but we would not describe it as an excellent watch because it keeps the door open when you wedge it underneath. A watch may serve many disparate purposes; however, the qualities that make it an excellent watch are those qualities related to its distinctive function as a watch: accuracy, convenience, perhaps beauty. Similarly, an excellent human being is one who acts to fulfill his or her function in a distinctively human way.

Aristotle (1941a, 3.1) and Aquinas (1948, I–II, 1,1)[5] emphasize two unique faculties in human beings: will and reason. Will is an appetite for the human good: through it a human being expresses a desire for his or her own perfection, or in other words, for purpose. As other human appetites (say, hunger) are satisfied by the attainment of their object, so the will is said to rest, or be at peace, when the human person attains his or her end, and is not at peace otherwise.

The will is a *rational* appetite; its movement toward the good is informed by reason. Reason deliberates about the goodness of ends, and about the appropriateness of various means to achieve them. Through action of the will agents choose both ends and the means toward those ends. In this, human beings are different from animals (and watches): humans direct themselves toward ends that they choose (Aquinas 1948, I–II, 1, 2). It is the deliberate direction of human action by the will, informed by reason, that gives human acts their moral character. It is the proper use of these faculties that constitutes moral judgment.

A distinctively human act, since it involves the combined action of will and reason, is essentially an act of human agency. In order to concentrate on those human activities that are the material for moral reflection, Aquinas distinguishes *human acts* from *acts of human beings*.[6] The distinction between the two kinds of action can be seen in the contrast between the statements "my beard is growing" and "I am growing a beard." The "I" in the second statement identifies it as an account of a human act (McInerny 1993).

An act is not a human act if either will or reason is deficient. An act that takes place against a person's will is thereby less than fully human; at least, it is not *that* person's act (it may be someone else's). Thus, human acts are characterized by a certain amount of freedom—we want to know why a person chooses to do "this" instead of "that." If a person cannot possibly do "that," then it is pointless to ask why the person did "this"; we will have to look elsewhere for an explanation. We do not ask why a person chose to be hit by a car unless we think he could have avoided it. If the person's will did not cause the act in question, then it is not a human act.[7]

Similarly, ignorance of the human good makes an act less human. Persons may seek certain apparent goods that are not in fact good, or may act without full knowledge of the goods that are promoted or hindered by their actions. This ignorance may result because passions (fear, desire) cloud reason, impeding its exercise, or it may be simple ignorance, easily corrected through better information or instruction. Of course, ignorance itself may be willed, in which case we might ask why a person did not learn something he could have known. Two of the Aristotelian moral virtues, courage and temperance, protect reason from passion.

Aquinas does not claim that most of the things humans can be observed doing are human acts. Sleeping, idle scratching, and digesting are not human acts, for example. He is interested in human acts not because they exhaust the possible types of observable actions by humans; neither does he claim that most of the things that humans can be observed doing are human acts. He places human acts at the center of his moral philosophy because human acts are the object of moral reflection—we can only exercise moral reason about those things we can actually choose to do (Aquinas 1948, I–II, 1, 1). Neither does the Thomistic agent refer every act (i.e., putting on socks in the morning) explicitly to his goals (McInerny 1997). Some habits may be human acts if they have been adopted consciously by the human agent, and are liable to periodic or episodic reconsideration. I may act to change certain habits if events make them less desirable.

Because Aquinas was a medieval theologian, a common modern concern about this action-oriented approach is its theological context, which raises the suspicion that his moral philosophy is simply an apology for Christian ethics. Moreover, critics draw attention to Aquinas's argument that the good life is ultimately oriented toward eternal communion with God. This suggests that Aquinas is irrelevant to those who do not share his theological vision. Perhaps it is irrelevant even to those who do, since few individuals can be observed in direct pursuit of the beatific vision, and much of human activity appears to be less than fully rational.

Aside from the observation that Aristotle, whose work is crucial to understanding this tradition, was neither a Christian nor a theologian, it is important to note that Aquinas kept separate his purely formal, philosophical treatment of human acts in general, and his analysis of the substance of good human action. Philosopher Scott MacDonald (1991) refers to this division as he defends Aquinas from the accusation that he has nothing to offer those who reject his characterization of the substance of the good life:

One common line of objection appeals to alleged empirical facts about what human beings actually desire and what ends they actually have when they act. . . . If Aquinas's claims were intended as empirical generalizations about human behavior or psychology, objections of this sort would be relevant to them. . . . If Aquinas's claims are about fully rational human agents, then empirical facts about human behavior will not count against them (pp. 39–40).

MacDonald observes that the formal (that is, general) definition of a human act need not specify the act's end. Human beings act for a variety of goods, about which they often sharply disagree. Aquinas's analysis of the human act begins with an analysis of its formal structure, and the "should-ness" implicit in that structure. Only after exploring its formal nature (Aquinas 1948, I–II, 1) does Aquinas move on to a discussion of the ends actually pursued by human beings (I–II, 2–3). The formal analysis is independent of the ends for which human beings actually act; we will draw only on the formal argument for the analysis of the ethics-economics divide. Thus, it does not matter what Aquinas thought the ultimate end was; it matters only that there are ends, that they have moral force, and that there is one ultimate end (we shall take up this last point in the next chapter).

The Thomistic characterization of human action as rational and goal-oriented bears a weak family resemblance to economic rationality. Although the Thomistic account is much richer than the economic account, as we shall see below, the resemblance is more than superficial, and is not accidental. Economics may be a black sheep in the family of teleological explanations, but it nonetheless belongs in the family. Jesuit economist John Piderit (1993), in a Thomistic account of economic principles, includes utilitarianism among the classes of teleological explanations. The utilitarianism of British philosopher Jeremy Bentham (1967 [1789]) was an attempt to give a scientifically grounded teleological account of human action to replace the Aristotelian account. For Aristotle's "happiness," Bentham substituted "utility," which was thought to be measurable and thus more scientific. The utilitarian project was eventually abandoned, since utility was not in practice measurable.[8] Even though Bentham's project was a mechanistic attempt to undermine the Aristotelian account of human behavior, substituting for the operations of reason and will the calculations of a pleasure machine,[9] the project nevertheless bequeathed to economics the enduring assumption that human action is goal-oriented and rational.

The resemblance of economic rationality to Thomistic rationality brings to light an important connection between rationality and morality that is often neglected in economics (Hargreaves Heap 1989; Anderson 1993; and Hausman and McPherson 1996 are important exceptions). First, discussions of morality assume rationality: morality in Thomistic philosophy is the analysis of human action, which by definition is rational and goal-oriented. If a person is not rational, then it is a waste of time to try to engage his reason in a discussion of the best course of action; if he has no choices or is incapable of making choices, deliberation is similarly useless.[10]

Second, rational reflection has a certain moral force: goals that have been chosen as the result of rational deliberation should be pursued in a reasoned way. In the Thomistic tradition, this statement is self-evident, and is foundational: the first precept of the natural law is that one should pursue what is good, and avoid what is evil (Aquinas 1948, I–II, 94, 2).[11] Moral obligations are rooted in a reasonable assent to seek the good. Some philosophers outside of the Thomistic tradition defend the precept as well. Kantian philosopher Christine Korsgard (1997) rejects the self-evidence of this proposition, and instead locates the normative force of ends in the choice of the autonomous rational person. According to Korsgard, you should pursue your ends because you have chosen them, and your choice of ends establishes your identity as a person. To deny the normative force of ends is to deny the possibility of self-conscious action.

Whether or not the normativity of ends is self-evident, the obligation is rooted in human personhood. One acts to pursue one's good because that is the only way to be successfully human. It does not matter if the good is narrowly defined (a methodological goal, say) or is the good human life in its entirety; if a person's reason identifies it as the good to be pursued, then he is under an obligation to pursue it. The economist's professional aversion to any deliberation about goals does not shield him from the inherently prescriptive nature of his own rational reflection.

Because rationality and morality are connected, the account of rationality adopted by the researcher will affect the account of morality, and vice versa. Although economic rationality and Thomistic rationality bear a faint resemblance to each other, the Thomistic account of human action cannot be based on narrow economic notions of rationality. Neither can one fully understand or appreciate the Thomistic insights on the positive-normative distinction unless one understands the much richer Thomistic version of rationality. Indeed, much of the difficulty in fully appreciating the factors that limit the autonomy of economics from ethics stem from the truncated account of rationality in economics. It is not enough, then, to point out the similarities between economic and Thomistic rationality; we must spotlight the important differences.

RATIONALITY IN THE THOMISTIC TRADITION AND IN ECONOMICS

The canonical form of rationality in economics is instrumental, according to economic philosopher Shaun Hargreaves Heap (1989). In the instrumental model of rationality, the goals of the individual are prior to the economic problem. They are stable through time, and hopefully well-behaved—that is, they contain measurable arguments, and display curvature properties congenial to mathematical analysis.[12] These goals, which go under the name "preferences," are pursued by individuals who seek to maximize them. All action is referred to these preferences, and is in that sense self-interested.

The economic account of rationality differs crucially from the Thomistic account in three ways. First, the ultimate ends of human action in the Thomistic framework are not practically measurable; it is not clear that they are even meaningfully quantifiable. Second, Thomistic agents deliberate about the content of their preferences as well as the means to satisfy them; the addition of the choice of ends to the purview of rationality transforms reason from a technical, abstract process to a very human quest in which human purpose and identity are at stake. Third, the need to discern the true human good in an environment of uncertainty and contingency requires rectitude of will, or moral virtue, as well as excellence of reason. The Thomistic virtue of prudence, or excellence in practical reason, is both a moral and an intellectual virtue. Thus the practice of Thomistic rationality is unavoidably personal; it cannot be embodied in a set of logical propositions.

The economic account of rationality posits goods that are measurable: leisure hours, hours of capital input, amounts of products consumed. The goodness of the sorts of things that show up in utility functions is certainly plausible, both intuitively and on empirical grounds, but there is an important class of goods which is not countable, and which is not consumed in the same way that leisure and material goods are consumed. These less quantifiable goods are not just unusual cases, presenting the odd challenge to empirical research and theory; they are foundational goods in Thomistic moral philosophy.

For example, take the good of friendship. How does one measure it? People do not seek friendship in ways that can be counted—numbers of friends, the number or dollar value of gifts, hours of time spent in conversation or in proximity. The fact that in one friendship small gifts are periodically exchanged, while in a second valuable gifts are exchanged, while in a third no material gifts are exchanged at all, is not informative about the relative strength of the friendships, or their value to the persons involved. This material incomparability is not simply evidence of the difficulty of making interpersonal comparisons of welfare. Even if these friendships were experienced by the same person, we could not rank them solely by the types and value of gifts exchanged. The smallest gestures of friendship (a brief visit to the sick) at times matter much more than grand gestures (the bottle of expensive scotch from a business colleague at Christmas). Indeed, any attempt by friends to quantify their friendship may itself endanger it, as they begin to quarrel over how much each has contributed, or as each begins to suspect that the other is interested in friendship only as a means of securing gifts or other benefits.[13]

Empirical measures of friendship can be developed, of course; in a pinch (and there are lots of pinches) econometricians are willing to accept poor measures of intangible goods rather than do without. After all, one can always caution the scholarly audience that, to the extent that the data are flawed, the results may be suspect. Nevertheless, the problem of treating friendship as a countable good goes beyond the difficulty, perhaps the impossibility, of measuring it accurately. Friendship is simply not consumed in the same way that material goods are consumed.

Natural law philosopher John Finnis (1980) identifies in the Thomistic tradition a set of ultimate goods (including friendship, truth, and life) that are not consumed, but "participated" in. Piderit (1993) characterizes an ultimate good as "an abstract good that individuals try to incorporate into their lives by performing some appropriate action" (p. 50). By this definition, friendship cannot be an *argument* in a utility function; it is a *principle* by which people organize their lives, to which they commit their energies. Friendship is not achieved, or even expressed; it is instantiated in a person's life through actions, through projects that themselves may be completed and measured. Nevertheless, one never achieves friendship in the way that someone may achieve a certain material standard of living.

Because fundamental goods like friendship are principles by which people guide their lives, and not measurable ends which can be achieved once and for all, they do not fit well into the economic account of rationality, in which goals are specified and measured so that the efficiency of different means toward those goals can be compared. Moreover, since the set of fundamental goods are all of this nature, many of them are available to everyone, regardless of income: although life is contingent on certain minimum levels of material consumption, the qualities of friendship and devotion to God do not depend on income.[14]

The second important difference between economic and Thomistic rationality concerns the choice of ends. In economics, the person's goals are given, described by a well-behaved utility function. The formulation of those goals is not part of the economic problem. In contrast, Thomistic rationality encompasses both the choice of ends and deliberation about means. The addition of ends to the domain of reason radically changes the account of rationality.

Humans must deliberate about ends for two reasons. First, some ends are proximate—that is, good only insofar as they promote other ends—and the desirability of a proximate end is only discerned in light of the ends it in turn serves. Thus, to know if the medical end "increase your estrogen levels" is a good end, a woman must evaluate whether or not its accomplishment will promote her health or cause cancer. The next chapter explores the order among ends and the implications of that order.

A second reason to deliberate about ends is that there are many possible ultimate (i.e., intrinsically good, noninstrumental) ends, not all of which can be fully pursued by any one human being. Thus a person must deliberate over the full range of ultimate ends in light of his overall goal of happiness— that is, a good human life.[15] If the ends of human life are the same for every person, then the only reason to deliberate over the ends of human life is ignorance. Those who are aware of their true ends will have to convince those who are ignorant of their true ends. Quite probably, those who are ignorant will also have to be convinced that those who claim to know the ends of human life are actually in possession of such knowledge, and are not instead in need of instruction themselves. As a result, even if happiness is the same for everyone, there is still much to reason about: the criterion for belief (including the degree of certainty necessary to establish the truth of a proposition), what sorts of evidence are admissible in the court of human belief, and the reasonable bases for trust.

The process of reasoning about ends is further complicated by the variety of ways in which persons can pursue happiness. Although each person has the same human good, generally speaking, each person must seek that happiness in a different ensemble of goods. There are many options. One might become a doctor, and promote the values of life and healing. One might instead become a scholar, and promote the values of truth. Then again, one might become a cleric, and promote the values of religion. Each of these avenues, and the many others, are open to the individual, but no one person can pursue every possible good. In economic terms, the pursuit of even ultimate goods like life, truth, religion, and friendship is characterized by scarcity.

The answer to the question "Which goods should I pursue?" cannot be answered in the same way for each person; its answer is inescapably particular. This does not mean that reason can play no part; on the contrary, the person faced with such a choice must reason about the particularities of his or her situation, and what they demand. The strengths and weaknesses of the person, his or her inclinations, and the circumstances (needs, opportunities, constraints) must all be factored into the decision. Such deliberation puts reason at the service of the quest for the ultimate human good: a fully human life for a particular person.[16] Moreover, the quest for happiness does not take the content of the good life as a given: the good life is in part constituted by the inquiry about the contents of the good life itself.

There are echoes of this conception of human ends, and the role of reason in discovering them, in the recent literature on the constitution of preferences. Economist Matthew Rabin (1998), in an outline of the implications of psychology for economic theory, notes that people have great difficulty even determining the content of their own preferences. Post-modern economists Arjo Klamer and Dierdre McCloskey (1998) insist that the content of preferences is discovered in argument; it is discovered in the course of life in community. These observations map easily into the Thomistic account of rationality and its purpose: to reflect on and evaluate human goods.

That human beings deliberate over ends is indisputable. The incorporation of that deliberation into an account of human rationality changes the nature of reason. Indeed, it is debatable whether economic rationality, which deliberates about means alone, even qualifies as an act of "human reason."[17] To maximize a well-defined, unchanging objective function, subject to constraints, does not require a human being—a computer will do. Moreover, an important question—why do we care about this objective function?—is begged by the maximization algorithm.

Reason that deliberates over means only, and reason that deliberates over ends and means together, will formulate the nature of the human quest in radically different ways. Philosopher Alasdair MacIntyre (1988, ch. 3) documents these two approaches to reason in the life of ancient Athens; each approach offers a different vision of the good life. When reason deliberates over means only, it concentrates its energy on efficiency in gaining what are taken to be obvious external goods: riches, power, prestige. When these external goods do not correspond to a true good (when goodness and riches conflict, for example), this limited reason cannot explore the conflict, because it cannot question ends. When reason instead deliberates about both ends and means, it naturally concentrates its energy on the pursuit of excellence, or virtue. A community that structures itself around the pursuit of virtue will take into account not only the human goods which virtue makes possible, but will also pursue those virtues which promote the formulation and transmission of human goods in community. Because it does not take its human good for granted, it does not lose sight of it and pursue material counterfeits.[18]

Hargreaves Heap (1989) asserts that a new sort of rationality becomes possible when deliberation about ends is added to reason's job description. Instrumental rationality (the sort of rationality assumed in economics) pursues specified ends, not questioning them, but seeking the most efficient means to their attainment. Hargreaves Heap's alternative, "expressive rationality," is the exercise of reason in determining one's purpose, in becoming the subject of one's own development.[19] He argues that instrumental rationality is an insufficient grounds for economics, and that expressive reasoning about ends must be incorporated into theory.

The moral problem set before Thomistic reason is not only more complex than the instrumental reason of economic models; it is also much more particular to the individual. The individual cannot simply refer to a set of universal principles for the solution to life's challenges. The practical challenge to Thomistic reason is not to universalize a solution to a moral problem, but to particularize it. Accordingly, the Thomistic tradition grants a central role to the virtue of prudence, which is the ability to identify the human good in highly contingent circumstances.[20]

Economists are averse to prudence as a necessary component of good action. This aversion is not accidental—the modern scientific mind is uncomfortable with prudence, for three reasons. First, since prudence "makes use of" other sciences, it requires a breadth of knowledge that is by its nature resistant to systematic analysis. It is radically transdisciplinary (or properly philosophical), since it places no limits on the number or types of disciplines and practices on which it may draw. The radical openness and breadth of prudence make it impossible to systematize.[21] Second, prudence is ultimately concerned with the particular, since the best course of action is always dependent on the particulars of the unique context in which the action must be taken (Aristotle 1941a, 6.8). Prudence is always applied; its applied nature runs counter to the scientific mind, which seeks general laws.[22] Third, although prudence is an intellectual activity, it is not purely intellectual; it requires a will that is ordered toward the good even in unique situations in which the intellect cannot provide clear guidance. Thus, prudence is classified as a moral as well as an intellectual virtue (Aristotle 1941a, 6.13).

The acceptance of the need for prudence does not necessarily make economics less "scientific"; it merely acknowledges that scientific judgment requires as a foundation a set of habits which are themselves nonscientific, which are developed in community, and which orient the researcher toward the human good in particular circumstances. Any researcher who values senior colleagues, not only for their highly developed technical skills, but for their prudence in choosing which topics to pursue and how to pursue them in effective, practical ways, implicitly acknowledges a role for prudence in economics.

In light of their aversion to prudence, economists defend instrumental rationality as at least simpler and more analytically manageable. A common defense of narrow economic rationality is a positivistic one: economics will adopt a richer account of rationality only when a richer account will help it to predict behavior better. This response misses the point of this book: to explore the positive-normative distinction from the perspective of human action. What is at issue here is not what sort of rationality assumptions are appropriate for economic *models*, but whether economists should employ such a restrictive rationality *in their own thinking* about their research. It may be entirely appropriate for economists to incorporate purely instrumental, unreflective maximizers into their models; it is another thing entirely for economists to employ the instrumental reasoning of *homo economicus* in evaluating the direction of their own work.[23]

Economists need not employ in their own lives the rationality of the fictional characters of their formal mathematical analyses. In my experience they often do. They exercise a narrow instrumental rationality, or at least aspire to, when advising students, playing faculty politics, and even in formulating optimal stopping rules for spouse searches. One can only speculate about the reasons for this adoption by economists of instrumental rationality in their own lives. It may perhaps be a result of economists becoming what they love; it may instead be a perverse sort of rational expectations, in which economists feel compelled to adopt as modelers the rationality they assume in their models. Whatever the reason, it behooves economists to act like humans in their real lives, and not to act like the characters in economic models.

There is no reason for economists to exercise instrumental rationality in their own lives as economists. Instrumental rationality is an assumption, an abstraction from the richer, more complex rationality humans actually employ. Economists are human, too. The goals that they pursue as economic researchers may not be quantifiable, but may instead embody principles of action which do not fit well into a utility framework; economists reason about the ends of their research as well as its means, and economists must exercise prudence in choosing the good to pursue in research when the good is not clearly specified. Economists must shake off a purely instrumental rationality in thinking about their own work, or at least not kid themselves that they can be instrumentally rational and at the same time comprehend the insights of Thomistic moral philosophy. They should employ a richer rationality even if they reject Thomistic philosophy, and simply want to be better economists.[24] One thing is certain: from the perspective of purely instrumental rationality, much of Aquinas's account of the moral structure of human action will be invisible. To fully grasp the Thomistic account, one must understand Thomistic rationality.

This introduction to the Thomistic account of the human act makes two general points. First, all prescriptions, methodological or moral, draw their normative force from the ends they attempt to promote. In this, methodological and other moral statements are similar. This similarity provides a starting point for a discussion of the relationship between ethics and economics from the point of view of human action. Human beings who happen to be economists act to promote certain ends as economists in the classroom, the lecture hall, and the office, and act to promote certain ends as human beings in their homes and the other places they frequent under their secret identities (some may have no secret identities). It is the claim of this chapter that they are doing similar things in both places, under both identities. My task in the next chapter will be to draw out the connections between the ends they promote as economists and the ends they promote as human beings.

The second point in this chapter is that rationality and morality are closely related, when seen from the perspective of human action. That good ends should be pursued is the first principle of practical rationality (or the first precept of the natural law, in Aquinas's words); furthermore, it stands to reason that one should choose means which promote one's ends, and choose ends which accord with rational reflection on the good life. Economists are poorly equipped to fully incorporate this insight into their intellectual toolbox; the relentlessly instrumental rationality of economic models is not rich enough to encompass the insights of Thomistic moral philosophy, which employs a concept of rationality that deliberates about ends as well as means, which is mathematically intractable, and which requires the exercise of the virtues.

NOTES

1. A third justification, often given in purely theoretical work, is that the applications of careful work cannot be fully anticipated, and will become evident only after it is completed. This is itself a form of appeal to goals, and to historical experience.

2. For examples of this third reason, see Finnis (1991) and Etzioni (1988).

3. Quoted by MacIntyre (1984, p. 119).

4. MacIntyre (1984), from whom I get the watch example, argues that, from the perspective of function, the fact-value problem disappears. If human beings can be observed to have a function, that fact can ground "ought" statements about what constitutes good human function.

5. The citation for Aquinas's *Summa Theologica* may be confusing for those who have never used it. The above citation (I–II, 1, 1) refers to the "First of the Second Part, first question, first article."

6. Evans (1977, ch. 6) makes the same distinction, between "acts" and "events." Events happen *to* someone; acts are done *by* someone.

7. According to Aquinas (1948, I–II, 6, 4), violence cannot be done directly to the will. To be forced to will something against your will is a contradiction. We speak of violence done to the will when a willed act is impeded, or an act that is not willed is physically forced. Thus a person who, in a moment of weakness, commits adultery, wills the act of adultery. On the other hand, a person who is dragged to a cliff and is thrown over does not will her death.

8. MacIntyre (1984, ch. 6) offers a diagnosis of the failure of utilitarianism as a teleological system.

9. For more on this point, see Hodgson (2001, ch. 6).

10. Simon (1990) points out that the concept of rationality involves questions of understanding and assessment. To call an action rational is to say that it is comprehensible; it is also to express a certain judgment of it. One should not act irrationally.

11. There is a significant dispute about the moral content of the first precept of the natural law. Grisez, Boyle, and Finnis (1987) claim that the first precept is actually premoral, and has no prescriptive content without a further set of precepts for practical reason, which they provide. McInerny (1992) asserts that the Aquinas's treatment of the first precept contains within it morally binding guidance. Bowlin (1999) claims that Aquinas was not trying to give "concrete moral guidance" (p. 115), either incomplete (as Grisez, Boyle, and Finnis claim) or complete (as McInerny claims). Instead, the first precept sketches "the broad outlines of human agency" (p. 126), and places boundaries on the arena within which the moral virtues operate to find the good in highly contingent circumstance.

12. Even theoretical work that allows preferences to change over time fixes the form of such changes in such a way as to make the analysis tractable. See, for example, Becker and Stigler (1977) and Becker and Murphy (1988). Of course, true indeterminacy in preferences cannot be incorporated into economic models; this is a crucial shortcoming of instrumental rationality.

13. Anderson (1993) points out that moral evaluation depends on the "decision frame" of a moral decision, and that the choice of frame is itself a part of moral reasoning.

14. An interesting line of research (Oswald 1997; Frank 1999; Blanchflower and Oswald 2000; and Frey and Stutzer 2002) examines the determinants of self-reported life satisfaction. Income is a determinant of reported happiness, but is by no means most important.

15. The human will, which is a person's appetite for his or her own good, by its nature seeks a complete good, which we call happiness. All human beings formally desire this complete good. An important question for moral philosophy is whether or not happiness defined in this way is attainable. Aristotle (1941a, 1.10) argued that happiness is attainable, but only through the attainment of the virtues, with a healthy dose of good fortune, and in the totality of a life well lived. Aquinas (1948, I–II, 5, 3) argued that one can be perfectly happy only in heaven, although one can participate imperfectly in happiness in this life, through the attainment of the virtues, which are perfected by grace, and which orient us toward our ultimate good. Despite their skepticism about the ability of all to attain perfect happiness, Aristotle and Aquinas attribute all human action to the pursuit of it.

16. Bowlin (1999) provides a thorough analysis of the nature of the contingency and particularity facing the moral decision maker.

17. Korsgard (1997) argues that, when ends are given by passion and are not the product of rational reflection, reason plays no practical role, except to provide rationales for the person to do what he wants to do, reason or no. The Humean, passion-based account of economic rationality is not really an account of practical reason, according to Korsgard.

18. MacIntyre (1990) gives a clear account of how the virtues are necessary to the maintenance and passing on of the Thomistic tradition, by enabling people to learn the virtues that make rational inquiry in that tradition possible.

19. Korsgard (1997) and Anderson (1993) appeal to this expressive function of reason as a normative argument for pursuing ends, although they formulate the role of reason somewhat differently.

20. See Bowlin (1999, ch. 2).

21. Collini et al. (1983) document the attempts to establish a science of legislation in the nineteenth century, which failed because of the indefinite (prudential) nature of the discipline.

22. Piderit (1993) contains an extended discussion of the applied nature of ethics, and its similarities to economic reasoning.

23. To the extent that economists assume that human beings are mechanistic, unreflective maximizers, it is doubly inappropriate for them to apply the rationality of their models to their own research decisions. Evans (1977, ch. 6), modifying an argument from Beck (1975), claims that an attempt by social scientists to apply such a mechanistic, instrumental rationality to their research decisions is self-stultifying—that is, such an attempt undermines itself. The process of predicting behavior is different from the process of deciding what to do. An economist who predicts what he will do given his preferences does not make a case for his action. A person needs reasons for his actions, not causal explanations.

24. Nabers (1966) makes a similar point about the study of the history of economic thought: historians need to study the development of economic ideas within the context of the values that economists have pursued, and how these values shaped and directed their work. In effect, he claims that the study of the thought of economists must go beyond a study of the analytical content of their models.

3

—⚭—

Multiple Ends and Their Order

When humans reason about their actions, they do so in light of their ends. As we saw in the last chapter, ends have normative content—an implicit "shouldness"—whether they are the narrow, methodological goals of a researcher or the all-encompassing goal of happiness, instantiated in a life well led. This normative logic is discernible even from within the instrumental rationality of economics, which takes ends as given. For example, econometricians should take actions that promote consistency in estimation, if consistency (and not robustness, or some other criterion) is their goal. Theorists should construct their mathematical models in a way that promotes a clear outline of their arguments, and the implications of those arguments. The last chapter argued that a purely instrumental rationality was not up to the task of accommodating the full Thomistic account of the morality implicit in human practical reason. As we move deeper into the Thomistic analysis in later chapters, we will need to return to a richer account of reason.

The introduction to Aquinas's moral philosophy in the last chapter was incomplete. To recognize that rationally chosen ends have an implicit normative force—a built-in *shouldness*—is one thing. One can admit as much, and still be left wondering how the pursuit of methodological goals, with their implicit normative force, can possibly be related to the pursuit of ethical goals, with their implicit normative force. If the multiple ends of human action are unrelated, then the normative force of ends does not suggest any relationship between economics, with its set of ends, and ethics, with its set of ends. In fact, the various ends of human beings, be they methodological or nonmethodological, are related. This chapter will outline the structure of that relationship; the next will explore the normative connections between the various types of ends.

THE MULTIPLE ENDS OF ANY ACT

Consider the following example. Your colleague is poring over equations on a pad of paper. You ask, "What are you doing?" Let us first assume that you are in fact inquiring about his *human* action. The answer "I'm sweating," or "Digesting my dinner," would miss the point of this particular line of questioning, since you want to know what he is *doing*, the project which engages him. If you want to know why he is sweating, or the state of his digestion, the question "What are you doing?" is inappropriate. He is not, properly speaking, engaged in a human action. In these cases, "What is the matter?" or "What is happening to you?" are the right questions.

If your colleague understands your question to be directed at his acts of human agency, he might give any of the following answers:

"I'm specifying an earnings regression."
"I'm trying to estimate the effect of schooling on earnings."
"I'm writing a paper for the *Journal of Political Economy*."
"I'm providing advice for Department of Education policymakers."
"I'm trying to increase the human capital of children."
"I'm trying to get tenure."
"I'm supporting my family."
"I'm satisfying my curiosity."

Each of these answers qualifies as a potentially intelligible answer to your question. What qualifies each as an answer is that each refers to an end of your colleague's action.

The context of your question alone will guide your colleague in figuring out which end you are really asking about. For example, if you are already familiar with the colleague's personal history, his desire to succeed as an economist, and the project on which he is currently engaged, then you are probably not asking about his big goals: supporting a family, getting tenure, publishing a paper on human capital. Instead, he will know that you want to know the particular end that directly engages his energies now, and he will answer, "I'm specifying an earnings regression." If instead you have just finished a description of your own projects, and then ask him what he is doing, then he may answer "I'm estimating the effect of schooling on earnings," or "Writing a paper for the *Journal of Political Economy.*" If you have just met him in a school cafeteria, know nothing about him, and you have been telling him what has brought you to this particular school or program, he may answer "I'm trying to get tenure," or "I'm supporting my family."

From this example it is clear that only ends can serve as satisfactory answers to the question "What are you doing?" Furthermore, there may be multiple ends for any human act. Your colleague may in fact be pursuing all of the specified ends at the same time. This multiplicity of ends makes possible the miscommunications that lead to the class of jokes about chickens crossing the road: a question about one type of end receives an answer referring to another type. These answers are funny because they are true but uninformative.

The multiple ends of any act are often related to each other; their relationship is not simply coincidental, due to the fact that one act happens to promote each of them. They are not related like spokes radiating from a wheel, connected to each other only by their common relationship to the act itself. The relationship among the ends is more complex.

According to Aristotle (1941a, 1.1), individuals act with two sorts of ends in mind. The first, a proximate end, is pursued not for itself, but as an intermediate step toward some other end. Most human ends are proximate. I adopt the goal of leaving the house in order to go to the store to get some milk. I set my alarm in order to wake up in time to get to the airport. I run a regression to discern the causal relationship between schooling and earnings. I would adopt none of these ends (exiting the house, a set alarm, regression results) solely for its own sake.

The second type of end is an ultimate end, pursued for its own sake, and not as a means to some higher end. These ends are self-evidently good. "Self-evident" in Thomistic philosophy does not mean "evident and accepted by all." Instead, a self-evident concept needs only to be clearly defined and understood to be proven. To understand the definition of a self-evidently ultimate good is to understand its desirability. According to natural law philosopher John Finnis (1980), the self-evidence of ultimate goods is analogous to the self-evidence of first principles in logic, such as "something cannot both be and not be at the same time." In logic, we seek the truth of a proposition in light of, and by means of, self-evident principles. In the same way, we reason about action by reference to ultimate goods.

Ultimate goods are the intrinsic principles of human action. This is why it makes no sense to ask what further end an ultimate good serves; most people will respond with a blank stare to the question "Why pursue friendship?" or "Why be healthy?" In reply, they can only try to make you understand what friendship is, or what health is, since if you really knew the nature of either, you would not ask why they should be pursued. Piderit (1993) argues that someone who rejects the goodness of participation in an ultimate value—say she denies that friendship is good—"is not interpreting [her] experience correctly" (p. 98).

To say that a principle is self-evident does not imply that it is somehow innately recognized by everyone, apart from their ability to reason practically. Ultimate goods, like principles of logic, are often discovered in the process of practical reasoning, and do not precede reason as pure intuitions. They are discovered dialectically; they are principles which fit when tried, bringing order to the rest of the structure of practical reason. One discovers them, perhaps, through the exercise of an intuitive insight (*nous* according to Aristotle), but it is not an intuition that acts alone, independent of the deliberations of reason.[1]

Finnis (1980) claims that the set of ultimate goods is finite, and common to all humans in all cultures.[2] For example, all cultures value friendship, and all value knowledge (even if not all value truthfulness). One need not accept Finnis's list, nor his claim that the set of ultimate ends is finite, to accept the existence of ultimate goods or their central place in the motivation and justification for human action.[3] The existence of some ultimate ends, common to all cultures, is evidence of our common humanity; philosopher Lawrence Simon (1990), in his discussion of the possibility of understanding the exercise of reason in other cultures, relies on common ultimate ends as a "point of common reference" (p. 36). He does not call these shared concerns "ultimate ends"; instead, he calls them "a set of interests or ends we share" (p. 36).

Aristotle (1941a, 1.7) and Aquinas (1948, I–II, 1, 7) claim that there is only one ultimate end: happiness, or human flourishing. It is important to see why this claim does not conflict with Finnis's claim that there are several ultimate ends; neither Aristotle nor Aquinas nor Finnis sees a conflict. To reconcile these two claims, we must make a subtle distinction between the ultimate status of an end and the practical necessity of pursuing it.

The claim that an end is ultimate establishes only that it need serve no further end; it does not close all deliberation about the desirability of the act that attains it. One is not compelled to pursue an ultimate end to the fullest possible extent. However desirable a particular ultimate end may be, the choice to pursue it (or more precisely, to make one's choices in accordance with the principle it represents) must be made in an environment of scarcity. One cannot participate in all of the ultimate goods in an unlimited way. The student who decides to become a doctor in order to participate in the ultimate goods of life or health thereby limits the opportunities to pursue beauty (say, through art or literature) or truth (say, through the sciences). Parents face the choice between the ultimate good embodied in their family commitments and those in their work commitments: the chief executive of a large nonprofit engaged in an important work faces unavoidable trade-offs between the ultimate ends pursued at work and those pursued at home. These trade-offs are part of the fabric of life; they are inescapable, although they are not necessarily tragic.[4] They are also unavoidably personal: each person, taking into account his or her strengths, weaknesses, and opportunities, establishes and develops (or destroys and undermines) his or her moral identity through ultimate choices made in particular circumstances. According to Aristotle and Aquinas, the rational, virtuous pursuit of a variety of ultimate ends constitutes the moral life (see McInerny 1997, p. 25).

In order to pursue a full range of ultimate ends, and achieve the appropriate balance among them, humans need a perspective broader than that of any one ultimate good. We call this perspective that of a complete human life, or "happiness." Human happiness does not consist of any single end. Human beings pursue a constellation of ultimate ends; happiness is the fruit of the thoughtful pursuit of these various ultimate goods. In this sense, happiness is the sole ultimate good. Nevertheless, it would be incorrect to conclude from this that ultimate goods like life, truth, beauty, and friendship are properly proximate to happiness, since it implies that they are pursued solely in order to obtain happiness. Their subordination to the good of happiness is not like other subordinate relationships among other ends.

Philosopher Scott MacDonald (1991) claims that ultimate goods like truth and life are proximate to happiness in a special way. They are not *means* to happiness; they are *constituents* of happiness. Happiness does not exist without them. Thus, one does not pursue truth in order to be happy; instead, pursuing happiness is identical to pursuing truth, beauty, life, and the other ultimate goods in concert. Both happiness and its constituents are ultimate goods. MacDonald distinguishes between weak ultimate goods (truth, life, etc.) and the one strong ultimate good (happiness). Both weak and strong ultimate goods are part of the same account of the good human life. Thus, both can be called ultimate, although in different ways.[5]

The small number of ultimate ends, at least relative to the large number of proximate ends, raises a question about terminology: why are proximate ends called "ends" at all? Why not call them "means," thus ensuring that they are not confused with the ultimate ends of human life? Proximate ends are "ends" because they are a distinct focus of human deliberation and choice. Both proximate and ultimate ends move the will, and each is deliberated about separately. According to Aquinas, the choice of an end and the choice of the means to that end are two distinct moral acts (Aquinas 1948, I–II, 8, 3). For example, a student may decide she wants to get a good grade in a class. This decision is distinct from a further decision she must make, to get a good grade by cheating or by studying hard. The will can be moved toward an end without being moved toward a means to that end. Willing-the-end-through-the-means is a different act of will than willing-the-end directly.

The neat division of ends into proximate and ultimate does not imply that the structure of ends is simple—a single strand of proximate ends each promoting the next proximate end, and the last proximate end serving the ultimate end. The relationship between the various ends of any particular action is often complicated: any proximate end may serve as a means for more than one other end (I may write a paper both to influence a policy debate and to publish in a top journal), and even ultimate ends may serve as means to further ends (I may seek estimates of the education-earnings function both for the sake of the ultimate good of knowledge and in order to advise policymakers).

The ends from the example at the beginning of this chapter can be organized into an end-tree to illustrate the relationship among ends. Figure 1 shows the tree.[6] In order to discuss the structure of the tree, we must introduce new terminology. We must distinguish between "ends further up" the end-tree and those "further down." The term "ends further up" includes ultimate ends, but it also includes proximate ends that, in their turn, promote other ends, and eventually, ultimate ends. For example, in figure 1 the end "publish in *JPE*" is further up than "knowledge," but is not further up than "get tenure." Ultimate ends are not the only ends that affect the specification and pursuit of any given proximate ends, since there may be proximate ends on the end-tree above any given proximate end.

Although simple, figure 1 shows some of the complexity that is possible in the structure of ends. Of particular interest is the place of ultimate goods within the structure of the tree, and not just at its top. For example, the good "knowledge" (of the effect of schooling on earnings) is an ultimate good, signified by ℧, but it also makes possible the realization of further ends that are proximate, such as "advice for the Department of Education" and "an article in the *JPE*." The presence of ultimate goods further down the tree will raise important moral questions in the next chapter. These questions focus on the degree to which an end that is ultimate in its own right (truth) can be put at the service of other ends. Of particular importance for economics is the concern that the pursuit of the ultimate good of knowledge may be compromised by its proximate role in the pursuit of other goods—that economists, in pursuing other ends, may misrepresent to themselves or to others the results of their inquiries.

This order among the various ends of human action is best described as a "hierarchy." This term has unfortunate connotations of abusive authority; otherwise perfectly reasonable people conjure up visions of robed clerics

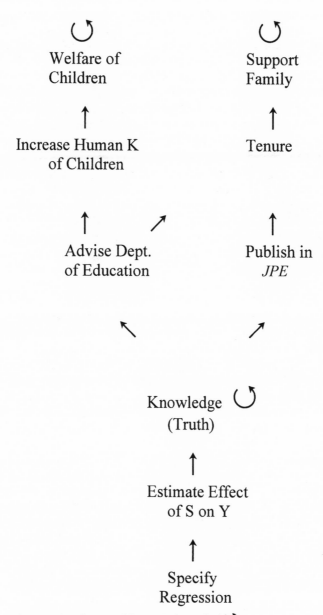

Figure 1. End Tree (Ultimate Ends marked ↺)

gleefully dictating to others the content of their end-trees. The word "hierarchy" may describe other sorts of structural relationships, of course, but emotional reactions to its use necessitate a clear explanation of its meaning and scope. That ends are ordered hierarchically means simply that ends higher up are prior to ends further down. By "prior to" I mean the following: the choice of proximate ends is justified by reference to the ends that they serve, but the choice of ultimate ends is not justified by reference to proximate ends. In the order of intention, the person wills the ultimate ends before willing the proximate ends which are the means to those ends.[7] For example, the ends of economic research are most often proximate; a change in ethical imperatives (ultimate ends or proximate ends further up the end-tree) may redirect and substantially change economic analysis, by pointing it towards a new set of questions or by redefining the nature of the human good to be pursued in an environment of scarcity. Of course, a change in the goals of analysis may not change the actions taken by the researcher, since different goals may motivate the same actions (McKee 1987), but the dependence of the proximate goal on ends further up the hierarchy remains.

This hierarchical language is frankly teleological because it looks for moral justification in human purposes. The teleology explored here is neither God's nor nature's, however; it is instead the researcher's. There is no need to appeal to a Creator, or even to believe in one, to admit the teleological nature of economic reasoning. Researchers who seek to further a certain goal (*telos*) will take actions and make choices that reflect and embody those goals. In other words, economic research is functional; the function is determined by the telos of the research.[8] Thus, this hierarchical ordering exists whether or not there is some authority external to the individual.

There is another way to explain the nature of the teleology invoked here: the hierarchical order described here is intrinsic to ethical reflection, not extrinsic. It is the formal structure of human practical reasoning, discussed in detail by Aquinas before he begins to argue for a particular notion of substantive good (Aquinas 1948, I–II, 1). Even a radically autonomous individual, free of any allegiance to external moral authority, gives evidence of hierarchically ordered ethical reflection, as long as he or she is rationally oriented towards some constellation of ultimate ends. The Kantian philosopher Christine Korsgard (1997) asserts that it is only the autonomous individual's choice of ends that can be the basis for the moral force of the injunction "seek good ends and avoid evil," since the individual's allegiance to the good embodied in ends is foundational to human identity and dignity.

Recent writers in the Thomistic and Aristotelian traditions avoid the use of hierarchical language, but describe the same concept.[9] MacIntyre (1984) uses the concept of "intelligibility" instead of "hierarchy." He critiques the loss of moral context in modern society, and the associated loss of a common moral language. Among the many things necessary to the recovery of a common moral vocabulary is the revival of the idea that life is a comprehensive quest for happiness. MacIntyre asserts that all human action is intelligible only with reference to the narrative of an entire life, considered as having a goal. The narrative of a life that aims only at proximate goals, without any overarching vision or plot, is not really a narrative at all. It makes no sense.

The French Thomist Yves Simon (1986), in defining moral virtue, takes a tack similar to MacIntyre's. While discussing what it means to do something well, he emphasizes the difference between "use" and "human use." To use something well is a narrow concept, appropriate to the description of techniques, which are defined by their proximate ends. Thus we speak of someone using his skills as a carpenter well, or his skills as an economist, if he pursues the proximate goals of his discipline effectively. In contrast, to use something "humanly well" is to use it in the service of a life well lived. The perspective of "human use" is the perspective of human happiness; it implies that an action can, and should, be evaluated in view of the ultimate good of the person.

If the project of this book were such that we might focus in a general way on the relationship of the quest for a good human life to the pursuit of the proximate ends that contribute to that quest, I might avoid hierarchical language, as MacIntyre and Simon avoid it. I might thereby avoid alienating those readers whose suspicion of human authority leads them to reject any hierarchical system. However, since the task of the book is to explore the details of the structure of ends that justify and motivate human action, I must employ hierarchical language. The vocabulary of proximate and ultimate, of subordination and superordination, is most clearly descriptive of the order of ends.

Before concluding this description of the structure of the human act, we must be careful to distinguish between an end-tree as a description of the human act and an end-tree as a model of human decision making. It is one thing to claim that, when human beings reflect on and critique their actions in light of practical reason, that the exercise of that reason reveals a structure similar to that of figure 1. It is quite another to claim that even rational human beings always make use of end-trees to decide how to act. The second claim is a species of instrumental rationality discussed in chapter 2, and is very close to the model of reason familiar to most economists. For this reason, we must explicitly disavow the second claim, or at least qualify it significantly, in order to avoid the mistake of too closely identifying Thomistic moral reason with economic, instrumental rationality.

If humans entered life fully informed about their true ultimate ends, and the means toward those ends, then they might reason about their actions in line with figure 1, by reminding themselves about their ultimate ends, and specifying actions that efficiently achieve those ends. If instead humans enter life as children, unsure of their ends, even unaware that there are such things as ends, then they will become aware of the structure of ends that motivate them to action only by reflecting upon their actions, under the guidance of parents and other adults. The development of a person's end-tree is a messy, dialectical process between posited ends and the means toward those ends; it requires patience and prudence, and as a result will be difficult, if not impossible, to systematize. In other words, if humans must reason about ends as well as means, then figure 1 provides a framework for reflecting on human action, but may not itself be a guide for human action, at least at the early stages of moral reflection. Indeed, the goal of human practical reason is to flesh out one's end-tree—to add or subtract from its branches when needed, in light of experience and reasoned reflection. Piderit (1993) offers a clear description of this dialectical "conversation" between ends and means. Only a mature person will be sure enough of his or her ends, and will have enough experience of the means toward those ends, to rely on anything like an end-tree in actual decision making.

The difference between the structure of reflection on human action and the structure of human decision making is analogous to the difference between a mature scientific system and the development of that system. A mature science lays out its theories of causation, the interconnections between its laws of motion, the primary components of the system, and the observed phenomena, in a tidy, complete fashion. This formal description is not, however, an adequate description of how the researcher builds and fills out the system, particularly in the early stages of a science's development; the process of reasoning and exploration in science is much more open-ended, even as it seeks to construct an ideally closed system. An ordered and complete exposition of its findings is a goal of the scientific endeavor; it is not the means whereby the system is developed. Only in the later stages of a scientific paradigm (perhaps in its degenerative phase) does the formal framework become a tool for the further development of the system.[10]

This chapter and the previous one have been a brief introduction to Thomistic moral philosophy, and its account of the human act. The previous chapter noted that humans reason about their actions with reference to their goals. These goals have a certain undeniable moral force: one should act in order to achieve one's reasonable goals. In the context of human action, reason and morality are closely connected, although the sort of rationality employed by practical reason is more complex than the instrumental reason assumed in economic models. This chapter has explored the hierarchical relationship between the various ends of human action. Upon reflection, the ends of human action can be arranged into end-trees, with some ends purely proximate to others, with some ends ultimate, ends-in-themselves, and with some both proximate and ultimate.

If economic researchers reflect on their actions, the multiple ends that they pursue can similarly be organized into end-trees. The ends that they pursue *qua economist* will most often be proximate to ends further up the hierarchy, although the ultimate end of knowledge for its own sake may serve as a proximate end as well. The methodological ends of the economist are always embedded in a larger context, a broader program of ends.

Two things are noteworthy about the hierarchical structure of the economist's behavior *qua economist*. First, even when the behavior in question (running a regression) begins in a purely economic context, the upper reaches of its hierarchy of ends rarely ends there. The hierarchy can end within the limits of the economic subject matter if the only ultimate end is knowledge for its own sake (finding the effect of human capital on earnings just because you are curious)—perhaps a defensible goal, but not usually the primary goal of policy-oriented economists. Second, as seen in chapter 2, the posited ends at every level of justification imply a normative prescription for action—it stands to reason that one should pursue one's ends. At lower levels (specifying and running a regression) we call these prescriptions "methodological norms." At higher levels (alleviating poverty among inner-city youth), we call them "ethical norms." Whatever they are called, they are implicit in the account of the economist's action at each level—one should attempt to achieve one's goals, whether the goals are specified at lower levels of the hierarchy, or at the higher.

Like all human acts, the actions of economists "doing economics" are ordered toward, and made intelligible by, a hierarchy of ends. The upper ends of this hierarchy are of an ethical nature, the lower ends of a methodological nature. Crucial to a proper understanding of the positive-normative distinction is the relationship between these ends. We will explore this relationship in the next chapter.

NOTES

1. See MacIntyre (1988, ch. 12) for an elaboration of this point.

2. Finnis offers the following list of ultimate goods: life, knowledge, play, aesthetic experience, sociability, religion, and practical reasonableness (or prudence).

3. See Hittinger (1987) for a critique of Finnis's list of ultimate goods.

4. The word "trade-off" is misleading. It does not imply that every ultimate good must be traded off against others. In particular, it does not imply that one should act directly against an ultimate good for the sake of another ultimate good. See Piderit (1993, ch. 3).

5. According to MacDonald, weak ultimate ends are subordinate to the strong ultimate end of happiness, but it is a "subordination of specification." Weak ultimate

ends are not simply constituents of happiness; they are specified by the individual who seeks his own happiness through them.

6. The idea of using end-tree figures as an explanatory device was suggested by MacDonald (1991), who uses them very effectively to explain the structure of practical reason.

7. Aquinas (1948, I–I, 1, 4) notes that the order of ends is reversed when humans act. In the order of execution, proximate ends are prior to ultimate ends. We seek proximate ends first in execution, to promote the ultimate end.

8. Jonas (1969) makes this point, and advises economists to explore the *telos* of actors in the economy (survival, welfare of children, etc.) as an objective basis by which to direct their research.

9. See also O'Boyle (1990), who gives a Catholic account of the relation of ethics to economics that is hierarchical.

10. See MacIntyre (1988, ch. 12) on this point.

4

—ᴍ—

The Ends of Economics in Hierarchical Context

In chapter 2 we investigated the common structure of reasoning about economic analysis and reasoning about ethics: both reflect on ends, and deliberate about means to achieve those ends. Moreover, the prescriptive force of both is grounded in the ends pursued. In chapter 3, we explored the relationships between the various proximate ends of economic research and the ends of human life in general. Economists do not live apart from the world, and the ends they pursue as economists are related hierarchically to the other ends they pursue as human beings. This relationship is not one of external authority; it emerges naturally from the exercise of practical reason itself.

The crucial question at this point of the analysis is the nature of the relationship between the proximate ends that an economist pursues *qua economist* and the ends of the economist *qua human being*. In other words, what does it mean that the ends of economics are always embedded in an end-tree, subordinate to ends higher up in the hierarchy of justification and motivation? What sort of influence do, or should, ends further up exercise on those further down? When, if ever, can we allow the ends further up the tree to fade into the background, even temporarily? Ultimately, is economics anything more than ethics? If economics is a branch of ethics, what does that mean?

Three principles in the Thomistic tradition provide the necessary background to answer these questions. The first, the "priority principle," affirms the inescapable connections between economics and ethics. Any

change in an end, ultimate or proximate, entails a change, or at least a reconsideration, of ends further down the hierarchy. It is impossible to sever
the ties of economics from its ends without destroying all rational justification for economics. The priority principle undergirds all of the assertions that human action is inescapably value-laden, including the claims
of the ideological and rhetorical critiques.

The second and third principles furnish a basis for a limited autonomy
for economics from ethics. The second recognizes that the pursuits of certain proximate ends is so common that they have been systematized into
"techniques"; the practitioners of a technique have formalized the choice
of ends within the technique into a set of rules and procedures whose purpose is the most efficient achievement of the technique's end. The practice
of the technique is related to ultimate ends only indirectly, through the
proximate ends of the technique itself. The technique may be practiced by
a different person than the individual specifying the end, thus allowing a
separation of the deliberations about means and ends. The third principle
addresses the presence within economics of an end—knowledge—that
makes unique claims on the researcher. Knowledge is an ultimate end,
and as such must not be treated purely as an instrument to other goals.
Because knowledge is an end in itself, economists are suspicious of any
influences (like pressure to get a certain theoretical or empirical result)
that may distort it, or which may cause it to be treated as a purely instrumental good.

PRINCIPLE 1: THE PRIORITY PRINCIPLE

The first principle simply recognizes the priority implicit in a hierarchical
ordering. Aristotle (1941c, 12) defines priority in the following way : A is
prior to B if B depends on A in some way, but A does not depend on B.[1] If
one can construct an end-tree for an act—that is, if an act is intelligible as
an act of human agency—then the ends which are further down the tree
are dependent on those further up, in the sense that they are desirable
only in light of the ends which they serve. In contrast, ends further up are
not dependent on ends further down in the same way; they are desirable
independently of the ends that are proximate to them.

For example, a researcher may decide that she wants to understand better the justification for some economic institution, say the International
Monetary Fund (IMF). In order to gain this better understanding, she constructs a game theoretic model in which an institution similar to the IMF
represents a cooperative outcome. The understanding of the IMF is prior
to the construction of the model, in the sense that she wants to construct
the model in order to advance her understanding of the IMF. The rela-

tionship between the understanding of the IMF and the construction of the model is not symmetric, however; her desire to understand the IMF does not draw its force from the model.[2]

Note that the claim to priority is not all-encompassing. I am not claiming that ends further up are prior to ends further down in every way— that ends further up are in no way dependent on ends further down. The claim of priority is a narrow one, involving only the order of intention, or motivation. There are other ways to order ends, in which the priority rankings are different. Take, for instance, the order of deliberation.[3] The range of proximate ends that are practically realizable are constraints on the achievement of higher-order ends, and so may affect the deliberation over which ends the agent wills to pursue. The availability and quality of data, for example, will affect the ends of the researcher, by forcing him to lower his sights if the data cannot be made to speak clearly to his most pressing research questions. In the order of deliberation, the quality of data is sometimes prior to the researcher's goals.

To deny the priority of some ends over others within the order of intention is simultaneously to deny the desirability of both lower- and higher-order ends; it throws into question the hierarchical ordering itself. The value of lower-order ends, like the ends of economic research, is thrown into question because these ends are obviously instrumental to *some* other good. According to Aquinas (1993, no. 23), "the reason for the means must always be found in the end itself," and a subordinate end is itself a means to some superordinate end. Why should one bother with research that promotes no higher purpose?

This need to justify economic research in terms of higher-order ends should come as no surprise to economists. All good economic research must serve some worthwhile purpose. Few economists need much convincing on this point, so I will provide only one example.[4] The most noteworthy proponent of the subordinate position of economics in the chain of ends is Lionel Robbins (1963), who asserts that the logical priority of "politics," whose subject matter is the higher ends of human life, over economics "is not in doubt" (p. 23). Even as he stands by his strict positivistic demarcation of economics from ethics (outlined in chapter 1), he notes that economics is desirable only because it promotes worthy ends: "Few become economists from mere curiosity; considered as pure knowledge, our subject, although not without its Faustian moments, has far less attraction than many others" (p. 7).

The clearest evidence of the priority principle in economics is the necessity that a researcher pursue questions with interesting "policy implications." However technically competent an empirical or theoretical study, if it does not further some higher end—sometimes knowledge for its own sake, but more often explicit advice, or a sharper perspective on some public-policy question, or at least theoretical and empirical tools for others who seek to analyze public policy—it is not considered good research. Similarly, a good economist is seldom merely *technically* good; rather, he applies well-honed skills toward ends that are recognized to be desirable. Even an economist who is blindly attached to his techniques gives evidence of the priority principle through his efforts to find practical applications for his models.

The denial of the subordination of the ends of economic research to higher-order ends not only calls into question the desirability of economic research; it also calls into question the desirability of the higher-order ends. It is the nature of ends further up the tree to be stated in general terms; as such, one can only participate in higher-order ends (such as "understanding the causes of poverty") by specifying and pursuing the ends which are proximate to them. Thus, the denial that a proximate end which can affect the achievement of some end higher up is dependent on that higher end in effect denigrates the higher end. If a person is really serious about an end further up the hierarchy of action, then actions and ends further down should not conflict with the higher goal.

As the above analysis makes clear, the denial of the priority of ends further up over the proximate goals of economic research is a symptom of muddled or incomplete thinking about the motivation for research. If higher-order ends are not granted priority, the motivation for the pursuit of proximate ends is unclear. Why bother with them? Left without a clear explanation, one suspects either that the individual treats the ends of economic research as ultimate ends-in-themselves, or that he has not reflected carefully on his own motivations. Rarely can this state of affairs survive close questioning, since most economists will not defend their work as an ultimate good; when pressed, most will point out its utility, however indirect, to the work of the field.

It is worth noting that the priority principle holds at any point in a chain of ends, not just at the top. Whenever the desirability of any proximate or ultimate end is called into question, the ends which are themselves means to it are also called into question, and may be abandoned along with it. Economists are familiar with this sort of priority from the deliberations about method within their own field. For instance, if the development of overlapping generations models as a means to understanding the phenomenon of money is called into question, then all of the ends which are proximate to the development of these models are called into question along with it. To cite another example, the choice of statistical objective affects the choice of estimator. The most common objective is consistency, but alternative objectives such as robustness or minimum mean squared error have also been defended, depending on the uses toward which the empirical results are put, and the resultant loss function. Different objectives in estimation will lead to different choices of estimator.

The priority principle plays an important role in both the ideological and postmodern critiques of orthodox economics (Myrdal 1984 [1954]; Little 1950; Heilbroner 1973, 1990; Wilber and Hoksbergen 1986; McCloskey 1994; Klamer, McCloskey, and Solow 1988; Mirowski 1991; Ferber and Nelson 1993). All of these critiques point out the connections between the models, operational concepts, and arguments that economists use, on the one hand, and the ends that they pursue, on the other. Each critique asserts that economists are only dimly aware of the connections because they are discouraged from examining the relations between ethics and economics by their training and by the positivistic, scientistic mind-set of the discipline.

Most economists accept that the ends which motivate their work shape and direct it, or at least should. The field abounds with examples: arguments about the relative social costs of inflation and unemployment spur research into those costs; to the extent that low income is an incomplete measure of poverty, other measures should be developed. Nevertheless, few accept that economics need be directed at every step by ethical ends. The sweeping nature of the priority principle appears to leave little room for economics as a discipline. There must be something more to the story. Surely, even if economics (and every other human endeavor) is a branch of ethics, it is not the same as ethics? In what ways is economics different from ethics and, as such, somewhat autonomous?

The sweeping nature of the priority principle causes two sorts of concern among economists. First, there is a sense that economics should have a weight of its own, able to resist the comprehensive rule of ethics. Economists fear that economics will become less objective the more it puts itself explicitly at the service of ethics. Moreover, if economics as a discipline becomes too responsive to the particular ethical demands of the moment, it may lose its utility as a general instrument applicable to a wide variety of social problems.

The second concern about the priority principle is that it is true, but that it claims too much. The guidance ethics imparts to economics is only of a particular, and limited, kind: the specification of ends, not research means. This is the claim that economics is technical, like engineering: ethics (or politics) tell economists what to produce, and they produce it to specification. Our tools and procedures do not vary with the ends chosen for us; they are only employed toward different ends. A clearer analogy is the archer whose target is chosen for him by an officer. It is true that the officer directs the archer, but only through the choice of direction and distance. Every other choice (gauging windage, proper aim, bow tension) belongs to the archer, whose rules of practice are unaffected by the officer's orders.

The positive-normative split abounds with these sorts of analogies: economist as engineer, economist as physician, and so forth. Together these analogies limit the effect of ethics to one dimension of the economics research problem: the specification of ends. The economist employs toward these ends techniques whose canons of practice are invariant to the choice of ends. Aristotle first provided the West with this sort of language—the language of technique.

PRINCIPLE 2: ECONOMICS AS TECHNIQUE

Aristotle (1941a, 6.3–6.5) suggested the first positive-normative distinction. The insistence that economic analysis is to some extent autonomous from ultimate ends finds its place in Aristotle's distinction between three types of intellectual activity: theory (*theoria*), technique (*techne*), and prudence (*phronesis*).[5] Each activity is distinguished by its end.

Theory has as its end truth (that which is); technique has as its end the making of an object or the establishment of a certain external state of affairs; prudence has as its end human action, and ultimately, the good life. Since prudence determines what we should and should not do, its exercise is the focal point of ethics; it governs the entire end-tree. Theory and technique are ultimately governed by prudence, but are different enough to have their own canons of practice, and can claim a limited autonomy from prudence.

Theory is intellectual activity whose end is unchanging truth, valued for its own sake, and not useful for some other end. For Aristotle, unchanging truth was to be found in the contemplation of mathematics, in the rules of logic, in the nature of divine beings, and in heavenly bodies (whose movements appeared unchangeable); for Aquinas, it was found additionally, and ultimately, in the contemplation of God, the source of all being. Economics as it was practiced in the eighteenth- and early-nineteenth-century heyday of the deductive method, in which deductions from "sure" premises led to "sure" conclusions, may merit the label "theory," but economics today employs a much broader method, whose claims to certain truth are more qualified.[6] Theory thus defined is not relevant to our inquiry, although the techniques by which knowledge is pursued are of direct interest.

Prudence is concerned with action geared toward the ultimate ends of human life. Its domain is the entire end-tree; it seeks the human good through action. As such, the ends of prudence are not expressed in external objects or states of affairs, but are internal, effecting the development and perfection of the person. Acts of friendship, religion, and learning, for example, have as their main result human development through rational participation in ultimate ends.

Prudence must deliberate about ends as well as means, both because it must construct the chain of proximate ends which promote ultimate ends, and because it must both discover and pursue in concert the various ultimate ends. This deliberation takes place in the highly contingent environment of a person's life, in which universal notions of goodness must be instantiated. The pursuit of the complete human good in such an environment requires more than excellence in practical reason; it also requires a will oriented toward the good in particular circumstances, free of the distorting influences of passions such as fear or desire. The necessity of both excellence of reason and excellence of will makes prudence a moral as well as an intellectual virtue.

Technique is an activity of the intellect whose end is the production of some thing, or some state of affairs. It is translated as "art" by Aquinas. A wide range of things qualifies as the object of a technique. The characteristic common to the artifacts of technique is their external nature: the technician produces something external to himself. Material goods (doors, musical instruments, ships) obviously qualify, but so do nonmaterial objects (mathematical proofs, regression results), and states of external affairs (market liberalization, a well-regulated public utility). Aristotle (1941d, 1.1) defines rhetoric as the art of constructing arguments. He defines the art of legislation (one of the skills needed in the practice of politics) as the art of making laws that promote the good human life in society (Aristotle 1941a, 10.9). "Technique" is broad enough to include what in modern English is translated as "art," "craft," and even "science" (Dunne 1993, p. 252). According to Aquinas (1948, I–II, 8, 2), both the building of a ship and its proper sailing are the products of technique. Even the method and operations of a technique can themselves be the object of a technique (Aquinas 1993, no. 1154). All that is required of a technique is that it produce some artifact external to the technician.

Although technique is concerned with a type of human action—"making"—both Aristotle and Aquinas distinguish it from human action in general, and treat it separately from prudence. Making is distinguished from other human acts in three ways: it works toward a clearly specified end, it exerts a high degree of control over its materials, and it draws on a formalized body of knowledge about making.

First, and most importantly, the practice of a technique requires a clear picture of its end. Techniques are developed through repetition; when a certain end is sought repeatedly, people begin to systematize its pursuit. Those who practice the technique may take the end as given; the specialist maker need not deliberate about it. Aristotle (1941a, 6.4) emphasized that technique requires only a very narrow sort of judgment; it proceeds according to a fixed method, toward an end predetermined in the mind of the maker.

According to Aquinas, the operation of technique is so automatic that it does not require the intellect to deliberate about its means—they are fixed by the method of the technique (Aquinas 1948, ST I–II, 14, 4).

Because the end of a technique is clear, technique is not a moral virtue (Aquinas 1948, I–II, 57, 3; Aquinas 1993, no. 1172). Unlike the practice of prudence, which requires a will conditioned to seek out proper ends when those ends are not clear, technique may be practiced by someone whose will is disordered by passion or injustice. One can be a good technician without being a good person, because a technician need not have the good person's ability to discern the human good (Aquinas 1948, I–II, 58, 5). Clearly, this separation of practice from moral virtue is desirable to economists, and to any social scientist who seeks a common, objective arena in which to develop his analysis. We shall take up the claim that economics is a technique in chapter 7. J. S. Mill's comment, "[A] person is not likely to be a good political economist who is nothing else" (Mill 1985 [1866], p. 306, quoted by Redman 1997, p. 349), expresses some doubt about economics' status as a technique, and the narrowness of its defined ends.

The second distinctive characteristic of technique is the high degree of control a technician exercises over his materials. He can wield the hammer, formulate an argument, or specify a regression without any resistance from his tools or his material. Hammers do not rebel against their wielder, and statistical software will consent to run even an uninformative regression. Contrast the control exercised in technique with the lack of control that characterizes the exercise of prudence. The self-direction that constitutes prudence involves more contingency, uncertainty, and interaction with sometimes uncooperative humans than does the making which constitutes technique. The differences in control may be a matter of degree, not type, but the differences are so extreme as to render technique and prudence different forms of intellectual activity.

A technique only develops when the end of the technique is repeatedly sought. The third characteristic of technique, the existence of a developed body of knowledge of making on which the craftsman can draw, can only come about when the first two conditions, a clear end and a high degree of control exercised by the technician, are satisfied. When a particular external end is repeatedly sought, the craftsman can draw on a history of making to formalize the technique. Whereas the human acts which are the domain of prudence take place in an environment that is always new and contingent, for which no exact formulas are available, actions defined as "making" are characterized by predictability, or at least a contingency whose proportions are well understood from long personal experience or a body of knowledge about making. Joseph Dunne (1993) claims that Aristotelian technique lies either in a body of knowledge that has been fully systematized so as to provide strict and ready-made guidance to the [craftsman] or—in the much more frequent cases where such an "exact and self-contained" science is not available—in a process of deliberation . . . where the [craftsman] has to inquire . . . about what is to be done—but where such inquiry can nonetheless be described as "analytic" in that it runs along tracks that are very clearly laid down by the (prior) possession of the form or end (p. 353).

The exercise of a technical skill requires a very narrow sort of judgment, which identifies an end and applies well-defined techniques toward its realization.

Although technique is a human action, and thus comes under the influence of prudence, prudence exercises control over technique only in providing it with an end—a person decides to build a table for his house, or a patient asks a physician for treatment to safeguard his health. The means chosen to achieve the end of the technique are chosen according to a logic internal to it, which draws on the history of the technique and the experience of the technician. Moreover, the guidance of technique by prudence is a testament to the necessity of technique: prudence needs the tools of technique to achieve its ends—a fully human life. To restate a saying of the French Thomist Etienne Gilson, prudence is no substitute for technique.[7] The prudent person must respect and master the ways of technique, if he is to be truly prudent.[8]

The classic defenses of the positive-normative split, from Ricardo's assertion that economics can tell you how to become rich, but not whether to become rich, to Robbins's distinction between economist and policymaker, claim for economics the status of a technique. Positive economics, by this line of reasoning, is defined as the body of techniques that have been formalized in the pursuit of certain ends—explanation and prediction of social phenomena. Such a claim seeks to limit the effects of ethics to the determination of the proximate ends that direct the techniques of economic analysis. Moreover, if economics is, according to its technical nature, directed toward proximate ends, then by definition it does not contain resources for more comprehensive prudential deliberations about ultimate ends. Its practice may be directed in light of ultimate ends, but it itself does not deliberate about ultimate ends. The status of economics as a technique, and the consequences of treating it as if it were a technique, will be a central concern of the rest of this book.

Notice that the classification of economics as an Aristotelian technique lends credence to economist Jacob Viner's claim that economics is "what economists do."[9] If economics is a technique, then it is constituted both by the ends economists tend to adopt and by its highly developed means. It is not "anything economists do," but "what economists have decided to do in pursuit of the ends of economics." It is also historically contingent, dependent on the sorts of questions that economics has pursued and the ways in which it has formalized its pursuit of the answers.

PRINCIPLE 3: ECONOMIC KNOWLEDGE AS AN ULTIMATE END

The claim for a limited autonomy of economics from ethics is reinforced by the presence of an ultimate end, knowledge, among the ends directly served by economics. Many of the techniques of economics have as their immediate object the making of some true statement—"the data reject the null hypothesis," or "the model implies a negative relationship between X and Y," for example. That economic knowledge furthers other desirable ends in no way affects its status as an ultimate end. The presence of this ultimate end among the ends of economics places on the researcher a set of moral obligations that are separate from the obligations implicit in the ends further up.

Because knowledge is an ultimate end in its own right, there are strict limits to its instrumentalization toward further ends: in seeking to realize goods further up the end-tree from economics, one must not act directly against the good of knowledge. In order to understand these limits, and their implications for the autonomy of economics, we must make a distinction between acting directly against an ultimate good, and acting indirectly against it.

The natural law ethics of Aquinas forbids any action that directly diminishes an ultimate good, but may allow actions that indirectly diminish ultimate goods. Direct harm is done when something good is voluntarily destroyed or marred by the action of the individual. Indirect harm occurs through neglect of an ultimate good; it results from actions not done. For example, a doctor may take time off from her job, thereby curing fewer people, and diminishing her participation in the ultimate good of health. The choices she makes with her time are of course morally significant: one may question the doctor's decision, and attempt to convince her that she should spend more time at the office, or even more time away from it. Nevertheless, her decision is not on the face of it obviously wrong. In contrast, a doctor who shows up for work and consciously works to make her clients sicker acts directly against health: her actions proclaim that she values sickness, not health.

The distinction between direct and indirect actions against ultimate goods asserts an asymmetry between commission and omission which is uncommon in economic theory, and which may be unfamiliar to economists whose approach to choice does not make this distinction. Acts of commission and omission may lead to identical budget sets in the economic theory of choice. For example, consider the budget set between goods X and Y for a consumer who has income I, no endowment of either good, and faces prices P_X and P_Y. If the consumer's income falls to zero, but his endowment of good Y increases to I/P_Y, the budget set will not change. Neither will it matter to the analysis if the consumer is offered P_Y for each unit of Y he destroys, instead of being offered P_Y in a market exchange. What matters is the trade-offs in final consumption implicit in the budget constraint, not the details of how one arrives at a particular point.

If goods X and Y were ultimate goods, it would matter very much how the trade-offs between them were effected, even though, analytically, the budget set might be unchanged. Economists may draw no distinction between direct action and indirect action against an ultimate value, but the distinction is very common in most moral systems. Destroying a perfectly good machine is not morally equivalent to failing to invest in it in the first place; deciding to seek fewer friendships is not morally equivalent to befriending and then abandoning someone; not taking action that might save someone is not morally equivalent to killing someone with your bare hands; not knowing an important piece of information that you should have learned but did not is not morally equivalent to knowing the information and misrepresenting it to someone else.

This limit to the violability of ultimate goods represents a limit to consequentialist moral theories, since direct action against an ultimate good is often justified by the beneficial consequences of increased participation in some other ultimate good. According to Finnis (1980), a direct action against an ultimate good cannot be rationally defended; since it cannot be defended reasonably, it cannot be a good act. Ultimate values are incommensurable: there is no rational way to compare the value of truth to the value of friendship, for example. Because there is no reasoned way to compare two ultimate goods, any trade-offs between ultimate goods are by their nature arbitrary and unreasonable.[10] Consequently, direct action against one ultimate good in order that another ultimate good may be promoted cannot be given a reasoned justification; it is instead an act of unreasoned power or passion, not befitting a creature of will and reason.

The rejection of direct actions against ultimate ends because they have no rational justification is characteristic of a class of natural law moral theories. Not everyone accepts this natural law prohibition; the natural law tradition, however, is not the only tradition that puts limits on the trade-offs among human goods. One need not rely on it to justify the special status of economic knowledge as a moral category. Etzioni (1986, 1988) argues that economic theory should take seriously deontological ethics, which results in the refusal to trade off certain values against others. Lukes (1996) gives a justification for the prohibition on trade-offs that invokes expressive rationality: human beings assert the value of certain goods by refusing to trade them off against others. Commitments to some goods, like friendship and truth, are threatened by the calculus of trade-offs. By rejecting the metaphor of trade-offs as a guide for decision making in certain cases, the person preserves certain ultimate goods.[11]

The application to economic research of the prohibition on direct action against an ultimate value is clear. Knowledge is undoubtedly an ultimate good. All persons desire to know, according to Aristotle (1941e, I.1); although some people want to deceive others, no one wants to be deceived (Augustine 1961, 10.23). Leonardo da Vinci's insistence that truth, not the nobility of subject matter, is the measure of a science's greatness, created the preconditions for modern science.[12] Of course, not all knowledge is intrinsically valuable—we do not value useless information such as the number of times the letter "q" appears in this chapter[13]—but we nevertheless place a special moral weight on the truth about the things we care about.[14]

Many economists suspect that to give ethics a role in economics will put economic knowledge at risk. In part, this suspicion is based on a long-standing suspicion of human authority, since ethics is often identified with religious authority: let ethics in, and mullahs and preachers will substitute their religious authority for economic truth. Apart from concerns about religious oppression (which are unfounded in modern Western societies, but which are nonetheless a common academic bugaboo), an appeal to the priority of ethics raises concern even when ethical deliberations are entirely internal and free from external constraint. If a person grants too much weight to the ethical ends further up his end-tree, he may be tempted to cook the books, to find results that serve his ends, even misinterpreting or misrepresenting results. The presence of ethical ends further up is thought to threaten objectivity.

Economists are understandably reluctant to compromise their commitment to truth, or to adopt shoddy practice in pursuit of agreeable results. Economist Samuel Weston (1994) cites this concern in his defense of the positive-normative distinction. He asserts that the distinction gives economists the freedom to ask questions, and find answers, that are uncomfortable, by providing space for debating the truth of a logical or empirical proposition separately from its ethical appraisal, and by promoting the norm of objectivity.

Aquinas (1993, p. 26–27) makes a similar defense of knowledge when describing the ways in which prudence (which governs human acts) directs both technique and theory. Prudence may direct technique and theory by specifying the realm of their activity—what should be made, what questions of truth investigated—but its authority is not comprehensive. Prudence directs theoretical activity (whose end is truth) toward the investigation of certain truths; however, prudence cannot tell theory what to find. It directs theory to ask certain questions, but cannot direct theory to find certain answers. Neither may prudence direct technique to deny the truths on which technique must rely to produce its output. This is especially true in modern science and social science, which make use of technique to render judgments about what is and what is not true.

The Thomistic treatment of the embeddedness of technique neither endorses a complete separation of technique from ethics, nor does it erase all boundaries between ethics and economics. This chapter has introduced three principles, which provide a foundation for the Thomistic perspective on positive and normative questions in economics. The priority principle places economics in an inescapably ethical context. Economics concerns itself (for the most part) with proximate ends: regression results, equilibrium conditions, etc. Because these ends are proximate, they can only be justified by appeal to the ends further up that they promote. To deny this principle is to suggest either that economic ends are actually ultimate, or to admit that one has not reflected on the justification for economic analysis.[15]

The other two principles attempt to establish a limited autonomy for economics. The second may be used to claim that ethical concerns are distant from economics, because economics is a technique. Hence, economics may hold its ethical ends constant, and pursue them according to a formalized method. The third principle makes the opposite claim that some ethical concerns, namely the concern for truth, are at the very heart of economics. Because economists value truth, they are obliged to protect their discipline from the temptation to be less objective in pursuit of other ultimate ends.

Together these three principles provide a sketch of the mapping of ethics into economics. It is not, however, the whole story; there is still much sorting out to do, particularly in light of the apparent conflict between the first principle and the other two. Clearly, an absolute boundary between ethics and economics does not exist. Nevertheless, there is content to the term "economist"; it is not a synonym for "ethicist" or "moralist." The next three chapters are devoted to reconciling these three principles.

NOTES

1. Aristotle (1941c, 12) provides five definitions of priority. This is his second.

2. Croce (1913, pp. 348–50) describes the priority of the ethical over the economical by noting that something may be economical without being ethical, but that something cannot be ethical without at the same time being economical. This way of describing the relationship highlights the potential autonomy of economics, while at the same time emphasizing its incompleteness.

3. Aquinas (1948, I–II, 1, 4) cites the order of execution as an instance in which the priority of ends is reversed. In the execution of a plan of action, one must often accomplish ends further down before ends further up can be achieved.

4. If you need more convincing, try Pigou (1950 [1932]) or Dwyer (1982).

5. Aristotle actually proposed five types of intellectual activity. To the three mentioned here, he added intuitive reason, which grasps first principles, and philosophic wisdom, which combines intuitive reason and theory.

6. Adam Smith, a product of the Scottish Enlightenment, reasoned deductively from premises developed through induction (Redman 1997, ch. 5), and both Ricardo and Senior defended this deductive approach (Bowley 1949). J. S. Mill (1965 [1848]) claimed less certainty about the premises on which economic deductions were based, and as a result could not claim certainty, but only tendency.

7. Gilson said, "Piety is no substitute for technique."

8. Croce (1913, p. 375–76) also makes this point.

9. Hansen (1991) notes that it is impossible to find where Viner said this. Reder (1999), recalls hearing him say it, and it is widely attributed to him.

10. Finnis (1991) argues that, although the prohibitions on direct action against ultimate goods appear to narrow a person's options, thus reducing the likelihood of achieving happiness, these prohibitions actually broaden the person's moral vision, forcing him to resolve the tension between the pursuit of ultimate goods in new and creative ways.

11. See also Anderson (1993).

12. See Brehier (1965).

13. 143 times.

14. Both Anderson (1993) and Bowlin (1999) make this last point.

15. Aquinas (1948, I–II, 1, 6) provides an example which captures the balance nicely. A man on a journey whose goal is point X by time t need not think of the end at every step. The traveler can afford to forget his ultimate end while focusing on any particular day's goals. Nevertheless, he is not free to go anywhere and do anything on the way, if he wants to arrive at X by time t. Thus the Thomistic tradition recognizes that economists are not ethicists, but at the same time refuses to accept a radical separation of economics from ethics.

5

—ᴍ—

Aquinas in the
Marketplace of Ideas

WHAT SORT OF BOUNDARY?

The three principles outlined in the last chapter allow us to sketch the boundary between ethics and economics. The word "boundary" is misleading, though; it signals a desire to clearly separate ethics and economics, a sort of jealousy over intellectual territory. If the priority principle has any purchase, then there are *no* inviolable boundaries between ethics and economics, in one sense; economics resides entirely under the umbrella—within the territory of—ethics. Furthermore, economics is not within-ethics-but-separate, a landlocked sovereign state like Mongolia or Switzerland. The intersection of ethics and economics does not equal zero; it equals economics.

The boundaries between ethics and economics are more like the boundaries between a bank's economic research division and the rest of the bank; the division exists, but there is no doubt about the purpose of the research enterprise, and the boundary lines are liable to be redrawn with any change in the organization's mission. Moreover, because the goals of the organization are different in banking and academia, the type of research that is undertaken in a bank is different from that which is undertaken in academia: it is shorter run, more tolerant of ambiguity, and more geared toward gaining an understanding of a highly contingent short-term environment in which one cannot wait for better data. In other words, *the purpose of the boundaries themselves* is to achieve the goals of the broader organization.

Accordingly, in one sense economics is clearly under ethics. Nevertheless, in another sense we still insist on some space for economics. Economists are specialists in pursuing certain ends that repeatedly arise: description and prediction of market outcomes, discernment of statistical regularity and (hopefully) of causation in data, and clear understanding of the chain of reasoning in economic policy arguments. Even a bank that closely controls its economists' research actions must allow them to be economists instead of accountants or marketers if it wants to utilize the insights that economics can offer.

The Thomistic framework sketched out in the previous chapter attempts to have it both ways. Instead of choosing one of two extremes (economics as value-ridden versus economics as value-free), it creates a certain dialectical tension between ethics and economics. It invites economists to question their methods in light of the ethical imperatives that motivate them, at the same time insisting that the prudential concerns of ethics are not identical to the technical concerns of economics; it also insists that a good economist should seek to live a fully human life as a context for his work. This more pragmatic approach to moral questions will produce research which, in its proper moral context, will be more effective in promoting human happiness, without sacrificing its properly technical nature. It may also work to the personal benefit of the economist, who need no longer deny his ethical nature at every point of his economic practice.

Economics is at the service of ethics; it employs its own methods, which are worked out at a certain distance from ethics, but even its methods are ultimately judged in light of the ends of ethics. This dialectical tension between technique and prudence is unwelcome in an analytical world, in which clear demonstration is valued over messy dialectical give and take. The tension may be avoided in one of two ways, each of which emphasizes a subset of the three principles of the last chapter over the others. The first way invokes the priority principle to dissolve all boundaries between economics and ethics. The second invokes technique and the inviolability of truth to cut economics off completely from ethics.

Economists are well aware of the dangers of the first approach; the arguments against the absorption of economics into ethics have been aired repeatedly over the last 150 years. Most economists resolve the tension between ethics and economics by taking the opposite position; in theory they admit the priority principle, but in practice allow it very little purchase. Because the relegation of the priority principle to practical irrelevance is most common in economics, this chapter and the next two examine the consequences of the radical separation between the ends and means of economic research.

Before turning to a critique of the modern separation between technical means and the pursuit of human ends, it is worth asking why the separation is so appealing to modern sensibilities. After all, it has not always been the case that societies have put a greater value on technicians than on philosophers and those accounted wise. In Aristotle's Athens mere technicians, who were simply instruments at the beck and call of others, were slaves, and considered unable to achieve a fully human life.[1] Because slaves did not direct themselves toward their own fulfillment, Aristotle doubted that they could be either virtuous or happy. Similarly, the wise and holy person was honored by Aquinas; mere technicians, who did not integrate technical practice and the good human life, did not act in a fully human way.[2]

In striking contrast to Aristotle's Athens and Aquinas's Christendom, modern societies accord their highest honors to "experts," masters of technique whose very mastery qualifies them as wise, or at least as close to wise as the modern world hopes to come. Modern experts do not claim expertise about ultimate ends, although experts on morals may claim a certain sociological expertise about what people claim are their ultimate ends. The high status of the expert reflects a reorientation of society from a concern with ultimate ends to a concern with proximate ends.

Modern societies do not eschew discussion of ultimate ends in the belief that ultimate ends are unimportant; they have instead abandoned hope of coming to even minimal agreement about what those ends are. Even a rough sketch of this loss of confidence in ultimate ends would have to include the effect of the religious schisms and wars of the fifteenth and sixteenth centuries on the credibility of claims to moral knowledge, the consequent instability of societies built on absolute claims to this knowledge, the rise of science and of the scientific method as an alternative to the philosophical pursuit of knowledge, and the rise of atomistic theories of society, in which the proximate ends of material gain and advantage play a crucial role. I can only hint at this sweeping historical narrative here. Barzun (2000) and Guardini (1957) are possible sources for this history. I am more interested in the results of these trends and the implications of them for the project of this book.

There are two important consequences of the loss of confidence in the identification and pursuit of ultimate ends. First, the moral life has been relegated to the private sphere. Since we cannot rationally resolve our disagreements about ultimate ends, and since disagreement about those ends leads to religious strife, there exists a general agreement that we must not argue about ultimate ends and their achievement in a moral life. If all moral judgments are mere opinion, why stir others up with fruitless and harmful controversy? We can only hope that we can build and maintain a social order without recourse to unattainable public agreement on any ultimate values.

A second consequence of the loss of confidence in ultimate ends is a denigration of the role of moral reason. Taking its cues from Hume (1955

[1740]), the modern mind is more inclined to attribute human action to passion than to reason. There are no ultimate ends reasonably seen to be ultimate by the light of human reason. Instead, humans are moved by passion; reason's only role is to deliberate about the most efficient means to satisfy the passions. Furthermore, the purpose of society is the satisfaction of these passions. A healthy political order balances them; it does not question, shape, or change them.

The relegation of moral life and moral judgments to the private sphere, the denial of reason as a common ground on which to debate moral questions, and the concomitant desire to limit the influence of ultimate ends in social life has created a social environment in which technique is asked to bear a heavy burden, foreseen by neither Aristotle nor Aquinas. Because one can learn and practice a technique without being morally good, one need not venture onto the contested ground of morality to apply or discuss technique. In describing or critiquing a technical project, one need not bring up seemingly unresolvable questions of morals or motivation. Given the modern world's aversion to ultimate ends, it is not surprising that researchers gravitate toward the language and value-neutrality of technique.

The dangers in the wholesale adoption of a technical vocabulary are twofold. First, technical categories may be applied too broadly: activities that are prudential, and thus fraught with moral import, may be labeled "technical" in an attempt to avoid moral entanglements. Second, legitimately technical activities may be wrenched from their moral contexts, and insulated from legitimate ethical critique. The next two chapters investigate these possible dangers in economics. Before turning to them, we must address another feature of the modern world that is relevant to the application of the Thomistic framework to the activities of economists: the market and its metaphors.

THE MODERN MARKET CONTEXT

The scientific, cultural, and political changes ushered in by modernity have resulted in a society in which the insights of Aristotle and Aquinas seem alien and irrelevant; at the very least, they want translating. Before the Thomistic tradition can be brought fully to bear on the positive-normative distinction, therefore, more must be said about the very different social contexts within which Aristotle, Aquinas, and modern economists write.

The social context matters because Aristotle and Aquinas each took for granted an intimate connection between the ultimate ends of life and proximate ends. The intellectual lives of the Athenian citizen and the medieval European scholar were animated by the discussion and pursuit of ultimate ends, within societies explicitly (if sometimes only officially) committed to ultimate ends (MacIntyre 1984). Because the connections between proximate and ultimate ends were taken for granted, Aristotle and Aquinas did not directly address the separation of technique from ultimate ends.

The Athenian citizen for whom Aristotle wrote belonged to a polis whose existence was justified, and whose governance was debated, by reference to the good human life of its citizens. The *polis* was the ultimate social arena within which the individual sought his perfection. Its governance was the subject of the highest of sciences, Politics, which governed all other sciences. To be virtuous was to be a good citizen, fit to participate in a society whose goal was the good life of the many.

The medieval religious for whom Aquinas wrote belonged to an integrated Europe organized around the pursuit of ultimate ends. Although medieval society was not a comprehensive polis—neither the Church nor the various states exercised comprehensive power over all of European society—in the medieval vision every aspect of a life well-lived, no matter how mundane, was a participation in the Divine life, fully realized only in heaven. The alleged connections between worldly technical pursuits and the beatific vision did not imply that mundane pursuits (like farming or tanning) should produce ecstasies of religious devotion; nevertheless, it implied a real connection of technical pursuit to ultimate ends.

The social context for the modern economist is neither polis nor Christendom; it is the market. In the narrative of exchange, persons do not in their actions participate in some larger cultural project; in the modern narrative, the attempt to gear one's actions toward such a project is fruitless, since society is not consciously directed toward ultimate ends. It is similarly fruitless, and perhaps harmful, even to conceive of society as oriented toward anything like a common good or end; society does not exist in the way persons exist, and is much too complex to be oriented toward anything. Ultimate ends are neither discovered nor developed within the context of a person's search for the good human life; they are a given, a constant of human nature to be scientifically observed, an assumed preference structure. They are to be pursued, not deliberated about.[3]

Within this society individuals pursue their interests, rational or not, through exchange. Exchange further complicates the account of human motivation. In exchange, persons adopt temporarily the ends of others as means to their own ultimate ends: the researcher adopts the ends of the granting agency or department chair, not as ultimate ends, but as means to making a living or increasing his status. As a result, an economist's identity as an economist is kept separate from his identity as a moral person.

The discussion of ultimate ends is discouraged within the realm of expertise and technique, and takes place, if at all, in the separate social spheres of religion, culture, or politics.

From this market metaphor comes two important criticisms of the Thomistic approach to moral philosophy. Firstly, economists do not behave like Thomistic agents, with fully ordered proximate and ultimate ends guiding their research actions. They are driven by passion (or preferences), not reason; they want to make a living, and perhaps a name for themselves, but do not want to change the world. Secondly, even if economists do act for ultimate ends, it is not necessary for them to adopt elevated, "altruistic" goals, like alleviating poverty or building community, in order for economics to contribute to human happiness. The field improves itself in much the same way that decentralized markets increase wealth, independently of the intentions of individuals to benefit the field, and in spite of their purely self-interested ends. Economists beaver away at all sorts of seemingly useless projects, in pursuit of very private ends. An invisible hand operates in the market for economic ideas to turn these seemingly selfish academic activities into social benefits.

The first objection is fundamental. If humans do not and should not reason about the good human life and about the pursuit of the ends that constitute that life, then the relationship between ethics and economics is coincidental and uninteresting, even when it is undeniable. Moreover, the denial of reason's role in investigating ultimate ends is implicitly a denial of moral judgments about those ends, and ultimately a rejection of any guidance for decisions beyond rules for efficient attainment of already specified and unquestioned goals. In light of such a denial, any philosophical system which seeks to provide a structure to practical reason can only be purely descriptive; it shows us how members of a passionate species make decisions, but does not purport to be a guide to decision making.

The Thomistic framework suggests two rejoinders to this criticism. First, if economists do not act for an end when they conduct research, their actions are unintelligible. One cannot ask them why they have made certain research choices and expect a complete answer. Their analysis is simply not included among the reasoned human actions analyzed by Aquinas and Aristotle. One can only invite them into the reasoned conversation about human goods, and hope that they will not continue to exclude themselves from it. Others are reasoning about human life and its purposes; economists should also.

This first rejoinder is essentially a declaration of victory, and is unlikely to satisfy most economists, who sense that the justification for their work is at least intelligible, and who are unfamiliar with the Thomistic vocabulary. To their credit, Thomistic philosophers are not satisfied with arguments that satisfy themselves but do not convince others, and so turn to a second, more helpful, rejoinder. This response encourages the economist to examine his justifications, and to find in them the formal structure of practical reason outlined in previous chapters, including the order of ultimate and proximate ends.

It is in fact hard to believe that economists do not reason about the ends they pursue as economists. Much of their energy is devoted to the justification of their research actions in seminars and in print. Reasoning of this sort must of necessity involve ordered ends, and at least some of those ends must be ultimate, that is, not valued for the sake of something else. The ultimate ends may not be as elevated as "curing world poverty" or "alleviating suffering"; they may instead include "becoming famous" or "providing for myself and my loved ones."

The ends that economists actually posit as ultimate need not appear on the list of John Finnis (1980): truth, life, beauty, friendship, play, religion, practical reasonableness. The Thomistic tradition is well aware that persons treat all sorts of ends as if they were ultimate. Indeed, dialectic about the moral life is made necessary by disagreement and confusion about the ultimate status of various ends. Aristotle and Aquinas both consider (and rule out) the possibility that pleasure, riches, and honor can serve as ultimate ends.[4] They would not have had to address the status of these ends if many did not treat them as if they were ultimate.

Aquinas recognizes that any number of ends may be put forward as the ultimate ends of reasoned action, and that, as posited ultimate ends, they necessarily give direction to human acts. Aquinas's formal (that is, general) account can accommodate a wide variety of ultimate ends. Disagreement about the ends of human action does not affect the formal structure of moral reasoning (analyzed in Aquinas 1948, I–II, 1). He cannot accept, however, that action without reference to any end can be intelligible. It may be that researchers are unwilling to admit that they are in it for the money, or for entertainment, and so deny that they conduct economic research for any reason. This denial simply cannot be true. If it were true that economists did not act like human beings when conducting their research, we would have no reason to take their work seriously.

The second objection that stems from the modern market context claims that the "altruistic" goals of economics need not be willed as ultimate ends by economists. The field of economics produces new advances and a deeper understanding of economic phenomena without any one person seeking that advancement as an end. Breakthroughs occur as a result of work whose author had no intent beyond curiosity, psychological compulsion, tenure, or promotion. In fact, the individual researcher cannot predict the consequences of his actions for the discipline well enough to guide them toward anything beyond his own welfare. It might even be harmful for a researcher to think too carefully about the ultimate effects of a particular research program; such an inquiry expresses a hubris about the ability to foresee the effects of one's actions in a radically uncertain academic environment, and may lead to grand, unfounded claims about the value of a particular research project.[5] As Adam Smith's baker need not directly will the benefit of the consumer, neither does the education researcher need to will directly the benefit of school-age children. It is not from the benevolence of the researcher that better economic policies are developed, but from his or her self-interest.

This is an important argument, because it places us squarely in the modern social context. Modern academia is populated not by Athenian philosophers, but by narrowly trained experts, who specialize in technique and "sell" their analyses to foundations, academic departments, private institutions, and government agencies. The researcher may help others (e.g., granting agencies) advance ultimate ends that are not his. What are the consequences for the Thomistic framework of this decentralized pursuit of ends coordinated through market exchange?

Economist Daniel Klein (1999) labels this optimistic account of academic markets as the "Great Faith." By appealing to the invisible hand in academic markets, economists avoid tough questions about the purpose of their work and the allocation of research resources among competing needs. The Great Faith is the belief that economists can do good by doing well (i.e., by succeeding as professional economists). If an economist who looks only to his own personal "bottom line"—tenure and promotion—promotes the good of the discipline unconsciously, through market mechanisms, he is thus relieved of the burden of ethically appraising his professional life. Klein criticizes the intellectual shoddiness of this unexamined faith:

> But economists have not, of course, actually done the economics that would be necessary to support such a view of their own "industry." Again, the problem is not that economists are going on faith and making value judgments—such is ineluctable—but that the implied faiths and judgments are so ill-considered (p. 19).

We can begin to outline the effects of market exchange in intellectual goods, at least in a rough way, by modifying the end-tree from chapter 3. Figure 2 adapts the end-tree of figure 1 by incorporating into it the ends of others with whom the researcher exchanges. This in itself does not constitute an economic theory of intellectual markets, but it points the way to such a theory.

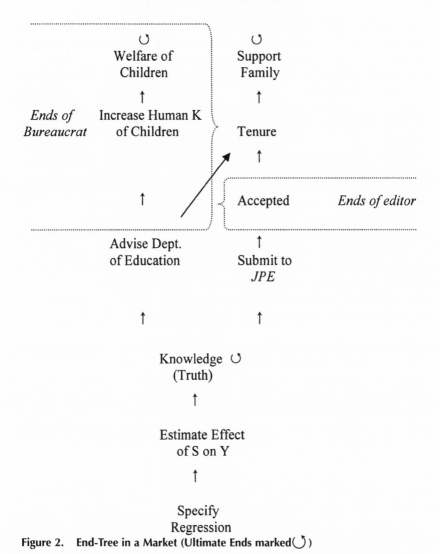

Figure 2.   End-Tree in a Market (Ultimate Ends marked (◡))

First of all, assume that the researcher in figure 2 cares only about his family's material well-being, and does not care about the welfare or schooling of children not his own. In order for him to achieve his goal of providing materially for his family, he must exchange with others; he needs to publish in the *JPE* and become a valued advisor to policymakers in the Department of Education. It is through his need to exchange to promote his ends that other ends become important to him.

One can grant the significance of the market and leave intact the claim that the "ethical" ends of economics still motivate research decisions. These ends enter the deliberations of researchers through the ends "publish in *JPE*" and "advise the Department of Education." The editors of economics journals want to publish papers which directly affect policy debates, or which improve the tools that economists use to address those debates. DOE policymakers want advice that will improve education policy. If the economist wishes to publish in certain journals or to advise certain policymakers, he must be willing to adopt as proximate ends the policy concerns of editors and policymakers.

Consider the researcher's interaction with the DOE policymaker. In return for economic research and advice about education policy, the policymaker gives the economist something of value: by seeking out and valuing the work of the researcher, the DOE provides a signal of the researcher's quality, and helps the researcher keep or get a job. The requirement that the research be valuable to the DOE policymaker inserts into the economist's end-tree the ends of the policymaker. The end "welfare of children" will be proximate, not ultimate, since the researcher only values it because it is an end of the policymaker with whom he does business. Nevertheless, "the welfare of children" becomes an end "further up" through exchange, and thus become influential.

Consider next the researcher's interaction with the editor of the *JPE*. In figure 2 we must replace the proximate end "publish in the *JPE*" with the proximate end "submit to the *JPE*." The editor makes the decision to publish, of course, so the researcher must submit something that the editor will want to publish. To do this, the researcher must adopt the ends of the editor as proximate ends, and direct his work accordingly. The savvy researcher will research the sorts of articles published under the current editor, or make use of personal knowledge of the editor's goals.

Even in the context of exchange, the Thomistic account of human action can find a place in these modern market descriptions of social interaction. It does not matter whether the end "improve the welfare of the next generation" is a proximate or ultimate goal of economic research. If an end has a place somewhere in the end-tree further up from the end "specify and run a regression," then it should shape and motivate research decisions. The account of the ways in which an individual's ends are developed in exchange, be it intellectual or market exchange, is richer than the Thomistic account of human motivation, but the relation between ends in the hierarchy of justification is left intact.

Although the Thomistic hierarchy of justification and motivation is still intact under exchange, the market complicates the relationship between proximate and ultimate ends by spreading the end-tree across a community. Individual end-trees are entangled with each other, and one person's ultimate goals may be only proximate goals for another, adopted only as an expedient of exchange. Although this more complicated relationship among the ends of many different people does not compromise the hierarchical relationship among ends, it does raise a new set of challenges for the identification of the proper goals of economics. These challenges may be analyzed in economic terms.

Because economists promote ends which are not their own, a market account of intellectual activity assigns a much greater role to the consumers of economic analysis: journal editors, foundation officials, and policymakers. These individuals provide the carrots and sticks that motivate self-interested researchers to adopt proximate ends in their research. A growing literature, surveyed by historian of economic thought Wade Hands (2001, ch. 8), applies economics to the production of "cognitive" outputs in market settings, with the goal of understanding how the structure of scientific communities affects the production of knowledge.

Of course, the end-trees of these consumers may be as or more complicated than those of economists. The DOE bureaucrat may be seeking his own material benefit in encouraging research projects which inform policy. He may care about the welfare of children helped by education policy only as a means of promoting his own career, or increasing his power within the education bureaucracy. Likewise, the journal editor may care only about increasing his own prestige by publishing articles of well-known economists, or currying favor with the advisers of the graduate students whose articles he publishes.

These egoistic explanations of the motivations of editors and policymakers are so common and expected in economics that I need not even fear that I am insulting someone by suggesting them. Indeed, my work would rightly be suspect in the eyes of most economists if I did not take these explanations seriously. What these egoistic explanations leave out is any role for "altruistic" ultimate ends like "improve the welfare of future generations." If altruistic goals are to play a role in the hierarchy of justification, *someone* must hold them to be goals independent of exchange—that is, as *his* goals, and not as someone else's goals adopted in exchange.

That the rhetoric of economic justification incorporates frequent references to the general welfare of both current and future generations belies the assumption that no one in society cares about altruistic ends. If markets for ideas are like markets for goods, then consumers of economic analysis must be sovereign. Even the assumption that purported altruistic ends are just talk, masking the pursuit of private interest, implies that someone with influence over the interests of economists must be persuaded, or fooled, that economics serves altruistic ends, and so must care about these ends. If no one cared about these ends, it is difficult to understand why

anyone would go to the great trouble of pretending that their research promoted them.

It is possible, of course, that a cabal of academics, granting agencies,
and policymakers has cornered the journals and government agencies,
agreeing to publish each other's work and to seek each other's policy
counsel based not on its policy relevance, but solely to advance each
other's careers. This would be akin to collusion in markets, and would
militate against the sort of socially beneficial research outcomes implied
by analogies with well-functioning markets.

This sort of collusion can persist even when noneconomists desire more
from economics than job security for economists. If the economic analysis
and policy cabals have information about the value of their research that
those outside of the loop do not have, a familiar principal-agent problem
arises; noneconomists may suspect that economists are running a scam
for their own benefit, but they cannot be sure. Neither do noneconomists
have recourse to incentive contracts to keep economists honest, because
any measure of the quality of outcome of economic research is bound to
be far too noisy to serve as an independent check on opportunistic behavior by economists.

It is certainly possible that economists and policymakers are in cahoots
against the general economics-consuming public; mathematical rigor may
not be a vehicle of clarity, but may instead be a convenient means of ob-
fuscation and intimidation.[6] Fortunately, the reality is more mixed. No
doubt, economics has some elements of a scam; I am often amazed that I
get paid to do what I do (especially on sabbatical) and I do not even work
at a research university. Nevertheless, I know too many economists who
came into the field in the hope of promoting altruistic goals (from alleviating poverty to promoting growth through free markets to arguing for a
more comprehensive social safety net) to believe that none is interested in
economics as anything other than a way to make a good living. Many, if
not most, economists mix a desire to live well and to gain the respect of
their peers with a desire to contribute to the commonweal.

If economists are in fact motivated by ends beyond those of material
wealth and academic prestige, then their end-trees contain altruistic
ends, some of which may not be their own, but which come from granting agencies, dissertation advisers, and tenure committees.[7] As noted
above, a market model of academic economics grants a large measure of
influence to these groups. Many of these actors are themselves economists; they at least cannot take refuge in their technique to avoid deliberation about ultimate ends.

One can grant that those on the other side of intellectual exchanges with
economists affect the ends adopted by economists without accepting that
those ends are the right ones. The ultimate ends promoted by an organi-

zation are the topic of crucial debates, and few can deny the possibility that those debates can be reasoned. It is possible, of course, that those ends should not be precisely specified—that the field should adopt a sort of laissez-faire, agnostic humility about what sort of research will in fact benefit society most. Even that conclusion requires rational deliberation about the pursuit of the good in economics, and evaluations of past research outcomes.[8]

The modern context of intellectual specialization and exchange does not cut the ties between the ultimate and proximate ends of economics. It is not without effect, however; it may well increase the separation between the formulation of ultimate goals and their pursuit via proximate ends, because those formulating an ultimate goal and those pursuing the proximate ends that are subordinate to it may be different people. Because Aquinas and Aristotle wrote for an audience whose pursuit of proximate ends took place within a social context suffused with and informed by the pursuit of ultimate goals, they do not develop an explicit critique of the modern insistence that the technique-driven pursuit of proximate ends can be divorced from the pursuit of ultimate ends. Although they acknowledge that people often pursue the wrong ends, and mistake proximate ends for ultimate, it would have been inconceivable to either that someone might wish to pursue a proximate end without any reference to an ultimate end.

Because neither Aristotle nor Aquinas develops a critique of the modern divorce of technique from ultimate ends, their framework must be developed to address this modern condition. Fortunately (and not surprisingly) there exist critiques of the modern dominance of technique. These critiques are not always Thomistic, but they can be used to develop a Thomistic response, to which we now turn.

NOTES

1. See Aristotle (1941b, 1.3–1.6) for a discussion of slavery.

2. Aquinas (1948, I–II, 57, 5).

3. Langholm (1998) notes that, over the last three centuries, increasingly impersonal descriptions of market processes further distanced the discussion of market outcomes from ethical judgements about those outcomes. Morally criticizing a market outcome became equivalent to criticizing the weather. Since market exchange was no longer described in terms of human motivation and action, it could no longer be the subject of moral reflection.

4. Aristotle (1941a, 1.5); Aquinas (1948, I–II, 2, 1–6).

5. Fonseca (1991) documents the rise of this argument *against* unself-interested action in markets. The argument is applied somewhat out of context here, to academia; it is nonetheless appealing to economists.

6. Baumol (1966) suggests that mathematical rigor may sometimes serve this function in economics.

7. Mansbridge (1998) argues from psychological evidence that much of human motivation is in fact grounded in something more than self-interest, and that norms of behavior cannot be explained by self-interested behavior alone.

8. See Hands (2001, pp. 388–92).

6

—〰—

Consequences of the Modern Separation of Technique from Prudence

THE APPEAL OF THE METAPHOR OF THE MARKET FOR TECHNIQUE

In place of recent philosophical arguments for ethics-free economics, which rely heavily on the logical categories of the fact-value distinction, the last two chapters propose a different, subtler defense of a less airtight positive-normative distinction. According to this defense, the boundary between ethics and economics is not absolute, but there is nevertheless a *technique* of economics, which holds higher-order ends constant, and which operates according to a set of procedures which are formulated independently of ethics. Economists specialize in this technique, and trade their intellectual product with others; these "others" determine the uses to which the technique is put.

This explanation of the relationship between ethics and economics can be misread in one of two ways. Each misreading fails to maintain the tension between the priority of ethics and the autonomy of economics, opting instead for one of two extremes. The first claims that, although economics may be somewhat independent of ethics in theory, it is completely dependent in practice. This is the position that economics has no real independence from ethics. Proponents of this position specialize in revealing the value-premises implicit in every economic concept, no matter how technical.

The second misreading goes to the opposite extreme: it claims that economics may very well be dependent on ethics in theory, but it is essentially *independent* in practice. The second interpretation is more popular among economists, whose training and professional norms are relentlessly technical and value-free. Most think that ethics is all to the good, of course, but that in the practice of economics they may ignore ethics. Economists are after all technicians, and technicians leave the direction of their work (the larger picture) to others.

The plausibility to economists of this practical declaration of independence is increased by the market metaphor, the conceptual context within which the economist's work is motivated and appraised. Economists do not work for themselves, so the story goes; they work for "others"—policymakers, granting agencies, journal editors, department chairs—and the "others" have the responsibility of determining the ethical values served by economic technique.

The classification of economics as a technique, combined with the market metaphor, is more convincing to economists than the fact-value distinction ever was, and explains in part the persistence of a strict, value-free positive-normative distinction even after the abandonment of the fact-value distinction. Economists are convinced of the *practical* irrelevance of ethics to their work for two reasons. First, technical issues take up almost all of the time of PhD students and research economists. The benefits of specialization in pure technique are too large to expect economists to devote resources to ethics. There does not seem to be *time* for economists to do ethics, so obviously someone else must take that responsibility. Second, the market metaphor is understandably appealing to economists. From graduate school on, economists spend most of their time developing and selling their technical expertise; a PhD candidate looking for a job is said to be "on the market." It is a small step from faith in markets for goods to Klein's "Great Faith" in an invisible hand in the market for ideas.

The technician is a central character in modern moral discourse; the metaphor of the technician selling his skills on the market is found throughout the natural and social sciences. There are resources in the Aristotelian and Thomistic traditions to develop critiques of the practical isolation of technique from prudence. These critiques are of two kinds. The first accepts the technical character of economic analysis, but denies that its status as a technique isolates it completely from ethics. Technicians are not innocent of ethics; because they bear some responsibility for the ends they serve, they must therefore concern themselves with ethics. This critique goes further, to caution that those who ignore ethics tend to exalt the ends of their technique, treating those ends as if they were ultimate, without having justified them as such.

The second critique questions whether economics is really a technique: a large class of the judgments that economists routinely make *as economists* involves the prudential consideration of ends as well as of means. According to this critique, economists must exercise prudence as often as technique in their work, and thus must place their technical work within the context of a full human life, judging the goodness of the higher-order ends served by their endeavors as economists. By this reasoning, it is nearly impossible to be a purely technical economist. This chapter presents the first critique. The next presents the second.

DOES IT MATTER WHAT THE EMPLOYER WANTS?

As an attempt to abandon responsibility for ethical reflection, the metaphor of the technician-for-hire does not succeed. The claim that economics is a technique, and the economist a hireling, does not let the economic technician off the ethical hook. Even the modern world does not completely absolve the hired hand from moral and legal responsibility for the ends he promotes for pay. Both accountants "cooking the books" for employers and soldiers "just carrying out orders" in atrocities are held at least partly responsible for their actions, even when they would not have chosen those actions if left to themselves.

Take an extreme case: an economist might provide advice to a criminal regime about how to commit genocide at lowest cost, in return for money which promotes his own ultimate goal, that of providing for his material needs. His actions may be consonant with his ends as he discerns them, but few systems of morals will refrain from condemning his abandonment of responsibility for the consequences of his advice. Even most emotivists will object, unless they happen to be unmoved by genocide.

The above examples illustrate that the consequences of our actions should affect our decision making, even if we will those consequences only because we are receiving a payment of some kind, as professional economic technicians. Are economists willing to reject this moral connection—to serve any master, even one whose ends are odious to them?[1]

Aristotle offers three examples of how seemingly value-neutral technical faculties are morally judged by the ends to which they are put. In *Rhetoric* (Aristotle 1941d), he distinguishes between the "rhetorician," who uses the art of persuasion toward moral ends, from the "sophist," who uses them toward false ends: "What makes a man a 'sophist' is not his faculty, but his moral purpose" (1.1). In the *Nicomachean Ethics* (Aristotle 1941a, 6.12), he distinguishes between "cleverness," which is the ability to "hit the mark," to actually achieve a particular good end, from "smartness," which is the ability to achieve what is in fact a bad end. Again, the moral quality of the faculty derives from the end to which it is put. In *Politics* (Aristotle 1941b, 1.8–1.9), Aristotle makes a moral distinction between the technique of "acquisition," which is a sort of household financial management, and the technique of "wealth-getting." The two techniques look identical, but are employed toward two different ends. We will take up this particular example in more depth in the next section.

Most people are unwilling to promote ends that they find morally repulsive; those who are willing, who are "only following orders," are justly condemned. More tellingly, most people (especially academics) are also unwilling to serve masters who appear to pursue *irrational* ends. An economic adviser, when asked to carry out analysis in the service of ends which his employer thinks are good, but which the economist knows to be harmful, will advise for a change of ends. For example, a desperately poor country that comes to an economist for help in creating a large industrial sector deserves to be told that its import-substitution strategy will harm it. Economists who believe that import-substitution strategies are harmful feel professionally obliged to advocate against them. If they advocate *for* them, then they are taking advantage of their clients. Few economists would publicly defend such opportunistic behavior, even in the absence of properly designed agency incentives (i.e., even when they can get away with it). Economists are supposed to offer more than knowledge; they are supposed to offer judgment and interpretation (Klein 1999).

In short, even if economics is a pure technique, its exercise can be separated from ethics only in the abstract—running a regression, deriving equilibrium conditions. But actual economic analysis is never carried out in the abstract. It is carried out as part of a project of action in pursuit of someone's (the researcher's or the employer's) ends; the evaluation of those ends has implications for the desirability of the research itself, however technical. The Italian philosopher Benedetto Croce (1913) makes this point succinctly: "Moral indifference belongs to them [technical actions], when they are on this side of the moral conscience, but within this conscience they lose the right to innocence" (p. 355). Moral judgments are never made about actions in the abstract; those judgments only make sense when seen in light of the actual ends served by a particular economic research project.

Claims of technique do not absolve the economist of responsibility for the consequences of his actions, even if he is promoting those consequences in exchange with others. Because even technicians care about the ends that they promote in the practice of their technique, in practice even technicians concern themselves with ends. If the ends promoted by the technician are not acceptable to him, he often will try to change them—either by refusing to work toward them for pay or other benefit, or by advising his employer to pursue different ends. Disinterested technical expertise, which takes no stand on the ends toward which it is applied, is a professional ideal but a practical, unworkable fiction.

MAKING PROXIMATE ENDS ULTIMATE

As has been noted, Aristotle and Aquinas would be puzzled by a modern technical neutrality indifferent to the deliberations of ethics. Although their work offers clues to a Thomistic critique of the modern autonomy of technique, neither addresses it directly. Of the two, Aristotle comes closest to such a critique in the *Politics* (Aristotle 1941b, 1.9), where he suggests that technique isolated from prudence tends to mistake proximate for ultimate ends. The *Politics* begins with a discussion of the elements of household management. Among the techniques necessary for managing a household well is the art of the "acquisition" of wealth. For the man who keeps the ultimate purpose of wealth (the well-being of the household) in mind, there are limits to the accumulation of wealth, since it is of purely instrumental value, and more wealth may not serve the ends of the household. Aristotle distinguishes the technique of "acquisition" from the technique of "wealth-getting"; the latter mistakes the accumulation of wealth for an ultimate, not a proximate end, and as a result sets no limit to acquisition. Because wealth-getting loses sight of the instrumental nature of wealth, its pursuit may actually harm the household's true interest.

The techniques of "acquisition" and "wealth-getting" are easily confused, since each uses the same method. They can only be distinguished by their end: "Each is a use of the same property, but with a difference: accumulation is the [ultimate] end in one case, but there is a further end in the other" (1.9). In this case, a hierarchical context makes a crucial difference to the practice of the technique.[2] The household manager who practices the art of wealth-getting is more likely to focus on the accumulation of wealth in the form of coin, and will "turn every quality or art into a means of getting wealth" (1.9).

Aristotle's example is an imperfect fit in the modern context; he assumes that the man practicing the art of wealth-getting has deliberated about ultimate ends, and has concluded (wrongly) that wealth is the sole measure of the good life. Similarly, Aquinas fails to address directly the person who deliberately focuses on technical, proximate ends alone. Aquinas (1948, I–II, 8, 3) notes that a man may become so busy with *means* that he does not achieve *the end* of his action. There is a presumption in Aquinas that such a person desires to reach the end through the means, but fails through the distractions involved in actually carrying out his intention. He does not address the modern technician, who ignores the choice of ends as a matter of professional integrity.

Thus neither Aristotle nor Aquinas fully considers the possibility of technique isolated from prudence. Each raises the possibility that one who is seeking ultimate ends may lose sight of them, or mistake proximate ends for ultimate. The modern expert, however, claims to focus entirely on proximate ends, without making any explicit claims that they are the ultimate or sole ends of life. Is the expert in danger of granting ultimate status to the proximate ends of his discipline?

Several modern philosophers who are sympathetic to the Thomistic tradition assert that the modern expert faces exactly that danger. The nineteenth-century British philosopher-theologian John Cardinal Newman (1982 [1852]) is the most interesting example of this critique, because of his timing. At the inaugural lecture for the first chair in Political Economy at Oxford, Nassau Senior (1938 [1838]) claimed that the new science of political economy was separate from ethics. Writing several years later, Newman highlighted the distortion that occurs in a field when it cuts itself off from the deliberations of fields of inquiry above it. He illustrates this distortion through an extended discussion of the new field of political economy, and of Senior's inaugural lecture itself.[3]

Newman accepts the existence of the separate discipline of political economy, in terms that should be familiar to economists:

> Of course if there is a science of wealth, it must give rules for gaining wealth and disposing of wealth, and can do nothing more .... Given that wealth is to be sought, this and that is the method of gaining it. This is the extent to which a Political Economist has a right to go; he has no right to determine that wealth is at any rate to be sought, or that it is the way to be virtuous and the price of happiness; I say, this is to pass the bounds of his science (Newman 1982 [1852], pp. 65–66).

So far, Newman says nothing to provoke an argument from his economist contemporaries. Indeed, this description of the boundaries of economics is strikingly similar to statements by classical economists David Ricardo and Nassau Senior:

> It is not the province of the Political Economist to advise—he is to tell you how you may become rich, but he is not to advise you to prefer riches to indolence, or indolence to riches (Ricardo 1953, p. 338).[4]

> But his [the political economist's] conclusions, whatever their generality or truth, do not authorize him in adding one syllable of advice. That privilege belongs to the writer or statesmen who has considered all the causes which may promote or impede the general welfare of those whom he addresses, not the theorist who has considered only one, though among the most important, of these causes (Senior 1938 [1838], p. 3).

The similarity of these three passages shows that Newman accepts the narrow definition of political economy offered by Ricardo and Senior. His complaint against political economy did not concern the narrowness of its chosen ends; instead, he criticizes the field for insulating itself *completely* from any guidance from ethics (for Newman, this meant theological ethics). This guidance is necessary to establish the scope of the discipline: "It [political economy] cannot itself declare that it is a subordinate science, that its end is not the ultimate end of all things, and that its conclusions are only hypothetical, depending on its premises, and liable to be overruled by a higher teaching" (p. 65).

When economists cut themselves off from deliberations about the ultimate goals of their research they inevitably substitute the goals of their discipline (wealth maximization in the nineteenth century and efficiency in the twentieth) for ultimate goals. Newman finds examples of this tendency to assign ultimate status to the proximate ends of economics in Senior's inaugural address. Even though Senior claims in that speech that the political economist must be agnostic about the contribution of wealth to happiness, at the same time he makes very strong claims about the contribution of wealth to human well-being: "The pursuit of wealth, that is, the endeavor to accumulate the means of future subsistence and enjoyment, is, to the mass of mankind, the great source of moral improvement" (Senior 1938 [1838], quoted by Newman 1982 [1852], p. 69).

Although Senior appears to think that this statement is trivially true, Newman objects to it in the strongest terms; clearly, it requires justification in an intellectual arena above economics. According to Newman, Senior exalts wealth beyond its role as a proximate end to human happiness, and does not even mark that he has overstepped the boundaries of economics in doing so, because he has cut himself off from the ethical deliberations which determine those boundaries.

Newman's point puts into perspective the periodic calls for what economist Martin Bronfenbrenner (1966) calls "defensible boundaries" between economics and other disciplines. These boundaries can only be established through the exercise of some vision broader than that of the disciplines themselves. A discipline cannot of itself determine its own boundaries. Even when disciplines are set loose to compete over their boundaries, as suggested by Nobel Prize–winner Ronald Coase (1994b), the relative success or failure of the methods of different disciplines can only be discerned on some turf beyond or above the grounds of the competing disciplines.[5]

This tendency, in the absence of reflection on ultimate ends, to elevate one's proximate ends to ultimate ends is rooted in human rationality: "Though it is no easy matter to view things correctly, nevertheless the busy mind will be ever viewing. We cannot do without a view, and we put up with an illusion, when we cannot get a truth" (Newman 1982 [1852], p. 57). Humans, being rational creatures, are under compulsion by their nature to construct an intelligible narrative of life, and intelligible narratives require ultimate ends. When they deny themselves the opportunity to discuss ultimate ends and the role of technical actions in a complete human life, they do not make do without ultimate ends; they are instead attracted to the proximate ends of their technique as if those ends were ultimate. They will accept a false but complete hierarchy of ends over an incomplete one.

Newman goes beyond his criticism of economics to note the naive overconfidence fostered by specialization. When a person specializes in one science, and does not participate in broader conversations about human meaning and welfare, he is like an "undisciplined talent," equipped with skills but unguided in their application. Along with this specialization comes an arrogance familiar in Newman's time and our own:

> Men, whose life lies in the cultivation of one science . . . have no more right, though they have often more ambition, to generalize upon the basis of their own pursuit beyond its range, than the schoolboy or the ploughman to judge of a Prime Minister. . . . You might think this ought to make such a person modest in his enunciations; not so, too often it happens that, in proportion to the narrowness of his knowledge, is, not his distrust of it, but the deep hold it has upon him, his absolute conviction of his own conclusions, and his positiveness in maintaining them. He has the obstinacy of the bigot, whom he scorns, without the bigot's apology, that he has been taught, as he thinks, his doctrine from heaven. Thus he becomes, what is commonly called, a man of one idea, which properly means a man of one science, and of the view, partly true, but subordinate, partly false, which is all that can proceed out of anything so partial (p. 57).

Reflection on the place of technique in the pursuit of ultimate ends functions as a practical safeguard against any unwarranted imperialism by economics, by orienting economists toward the broader ends served by economics. The point here is not that economists must bear ultimate goods explicitly in mind at every turn of their work. The danger of technique, however, is that its practitioners may lose sight of the ultimate ends that justify their work and pursue a proximate goal for its own sake. The antidote to this tendency is for economists to come up for air regularly, to participate in deliberations about human goods, and to conduct their research in light of those deliberations.

The narrow vision of the technician, and the raising up of the products of that vision to ultimate status, is one of the themes of modernity. German philosopher Martin Heidegger, in the essay "The Question Concerning Technology" (1977, ch. 7), cautions that modern technology, which he defines broadly as a method of "revealing" truth, threatens to get away from mankind, becoming not an instrument, but an end in itself, which orders, or "sets upon," man himself, apart from man's willing it. According to Heidegger, we can fend off our own domination by technology only by broadly cultivating other means of "revealing," like art.

That means may illegitimately become ultimate ends is a widely recognized possibility; Thomistic ethics is not alone in pointing it out. Several economists have addressed this exaltation of the means of economic research to the status of ends, and have speculated about the causes of that exaltation. Frank Graham (1999 [1942]), a mid-century critic of value-free economics, echoes the analysis of Newman, pointing out that economists do not reflect on the ultimate ends of their research, and as a result tend to treat the analysis itself as an ultimate end:

> Much first-rate analytical skill and much scholarly industry has miscarried because the road to academic recognition lay in the refinement of traditional technique, or in assiduous dust-gathering, with little consideration of ultimate purpose. The means have been exalted over the ends, and the neophyte, compelled to show his mastery of the technique, has quickly learned to love and practice it for its own sake (p. 29).

The modern economics student (even as far back as 1942, when Graham wrote), trained in an ethical void, is quickly stripped of the intellectual tools by which economics is placed in its ethical context. The pressures of comprehensive and oral examinations on technical subjects, followed by the need to produce a highly technical thesis expressed in professional, value-free language, produce technically isolated economists who are susceptible to the dangers Graham and Newman point out. More recently, economists Arjo Klamer and David Colander (1990) document the effects of this formal training on the attitudes of young economists.[6]

I am not suggesting that economics programs abandon technical training, only that they need not be founded on the academic fiction that economics can completely ignore ethics without any consequences to its social usefulness. It is true that ethics is no substitute for technique, but young economists are not at risk of making such a substitution. Instead, they face the opposite mistake, attempting to substitute technique for ethics.

The myopic focus on method, once trained into economists, is kept there by the pressures of publication in highly technical journals, most of which are repulsed by any whiff of ethics. Lawrence Nabers (1966) suggests another reason for the economist's unwillingness to look deeply at the ethical roots of his work. "The tendency to place a higher valuation or

greater importance on products on which much labor has been bestowed"
(p. 69) makes it more difficult to question the basic direction of one's research—its underlying assumptions, its concepts, its operational vari-
ables. It is not surprising that academics love their methods and models;
we tend to love the works of our hands, and resist any suggestion that
they are less useful than they might be.

Economist William Baumol (1966) suggests two reasons for economists'
attachment to mathematical technique (beyond its usefulness in modeling
clearly): it is self-indulgent, undertaken for its own sake, and it makes
noneconomists more reliant on the skills of economists, who must trans-
late obscure mathematical insights into everyday language. The first reason is consonant with the discussion of this chapter; the second suggests
a mechanism by which economists can enforce collusion of the sort mentioned in the last chapter: by speaking in a highly formal language, they
are able to keep the principals who hire them (policymakers, granting
agencies) in the dark about the quality of their analysis.

Benedetto Croce (1913), the Italian philosopher of aesthetics and
morals, sounds a compelling warning about the dangers from the moral
isolation of technique. In the course of an extended reflection on the separation of technique from prudence, he outlines three consequences of the
practice of technique outside of any ethical context.[7] He does not describe
the consequences in terms of the confusion of proximate and ultimate
ends; instead, he describes the confusion between the technical perspective and the prudential perspective, that of life conceived of as a whole.
His observations, even though they were written before the high tide of
positivist technique in economics, accurately describe the consequences
of the denial of ultimate ends in the field.

The first consequence of the complete separation of economic technique
from prudence is the negation of prudence, and of prudence's philosophical underpinnings. Croce notes that those who focus exclusively on the
technical do not just ignore ethics; they actively denigrate it as empty meta-
physical chatter, seeking to replace mushy prudential talk about ultimate
ends with the hard empirical methods of technique. Those who denigrate
prudential philosophy "do not merely wish to subdue but altogether to de-
stroy [it], substituting for it the methods of empirical observation and of
mathematical construction, thus favoring a particular empirical and mathematical philosophy of their own, however much they may protest to the
contrary" (pp. 384–85). Croce argues that the isolated technician cannot
help but put forward the ends and methods of his technique as a substitute
for the ultimate ends, even as the technician belittles the pursuit of ultimate
goods. As Newman points out, "the busy mind will be ever viewing."

Croce's second consequence of the separation of technique from prudence is the attribution of universal value to the narrow concepts and

proximate ends of technique. He concurs with Newman that political economy often identifies its measures of wealth with human happiness. As an example, he cites arguments against restrictions on trade which appeal entirely to their effects on national income. Although this argument is not entirely fair to economists, who (at least recently) clearly recognize that noneconomic concerns like national defense and the protection of employment in import-competing sectors may justify restraints on trade, it makes the defensible point that it is easy to slip into the habit of thinking of human welfare in terms of material wealth, instead of in terms of ultimate goods which, being principles of human action, are notoriously difficult to measure.

A third concern of Croce's echoes those of philosophers Margaret Radin (1996) and Elizabeth Anderson (1993), of sociologist Amitai Etzioni (1988), of economists Gerald Marwell and Ruth Ames (1981), and of others who worry that the language of economics changes the way persons conceive of themselves and their interactions with others in society. If the prudential pursuit of ultimate ends is ridiculed and then abandoned in favor of the more narrowly defined pursuit of proximate goods—according to the technical logic of maximization—it is not surprising that people come to view all of the pursuits of life in terms of the calculus of maximization, or the self-interested negotiation of contracts. Calculation replaces philosophy, and prudence is redefined as self-interest maximization: "The comparisons, metaphors, and symbols, taken from Economy and used in ordinary conversation, lead to the false belief that mathematical constructions and those of the economic calculus are the real processes of the psyche or of the Spirit" (Croce 1913, p. 388).

G. K. Chesterton (1908, p. 53) noted that the modern world's unregulated vices do not do nearly so much damage as its unregulated virtues. Croce's analysis clearly summarizes the consequences of the unmooring of technical practice from ethical reflection. Technique that is undisciplined by reflection on ultimate purposes will turn to good only accidentally, and may turn on its practitioners. Croce's analysis, written close in time to Chesterton's insight, outlines the ways in which unreflective technique "sets upon" the technical economist and the society in which he practices. It denies the prudence that might guide it, and it seeks to replace prudence with its own version of maximization. In the process it changes society's self-understanding from "human persons seeking the good in community" to "a collection of autonomous individuals satisfying their passions."

The critiques of this chapter take seriously the claim that economics is a technique. No doubt, much of what is taught in economics departments *is* technique; its status as a technique grants to it some insulation from reflection on ultimate ends. This insulation cannot be total, however, even if economists do not choose the ultimate ends served by their research, but simply work for pay or prestige. This chapter argues that even technique must self-consciously engage ethics, for two reasons.

First, technical pursuits participate in the moral goodness or badness of the purposes to which they are put. This is true even if the technical economist is hired, and the ends he promotes are not, strictly speaking, his. Just as we hold legally accountable those employees who knowingly break the law in the service of their employers, we hold ourselves and others morally accountable for even technical actions taken in a morally suspect cause. Many physicists who worked on the atomic bomb struggled with their instrumental roles; few found comfort in the realization that "I was only doing my job." Moreover, we are expected to engage our employers about the rationality of the goals they want our help to pursue. Rational debates of this sort are morally charged. The economist who does not question goals that he thinks are highly questionable, but instead settles for taking payment, shutting his mouth, and allowing the employer to achieve a goal that is ill-advised, will not brag to colleagues about the advantage he takes of gullible clients. He will hide his actions from them.

Second, those who attempt to practice technique as if its goals need not be connected to the good human life are liable to treat the narrow ends and methods of their technique as if they were ultimate. Narrowly technical economists, who refuse to be drawn into broader debates about their purposes in the discipline, may end up treating their discipline as if it were its own purpose. The method of economics becomes the measure of other sciences, and even of philosophy; imperfect measures of material welfare become the standards of human welfare, and all of human life becomes a marketplace: the family a firm, and the person an automaton, a walking maximizing algorithm. This absorption of ethics by economics does not bear close scrutiny. Economists must ask themselves what their techniques are for, and take the answers seriously.

All of this takes the claim of economics to be a technique seriously. In the next chapter, we will take up the issue of whether this claim is justified. In the messy practice of economics, beyond lecture and textbook, economics begins to look something like prudence. Accordingly, its practice cannot be separated easily from ethics.

NOTES

1. See Roy (1988) for a discussion of this point.
2. The exclusive focus on wealth accumulation as an ultimate end is fostered by the use of money as a medium of exchange, according to Aristotle.
3. See Oslington (2001) for an extended discussion of Newman and Senior.

4. Quoted by Redman (1997, p. 303).

5. Polanyi (1959) makes a related point, that "dismemberment of a comprehensive entity produces incomprehension of it and in this sense the entity is logically unspecifiable in terms of its particulars" (p. 45). One needs a comprehensive view of the whole in order to weigh the roles of the various parts.

6. See also Leijonhufvud (1981) and Leamer (1983) for notable criticism of the ways in which technical concerns cause economists to lose sight of their real objectives.

7. Croce contrasts what he calls "economic" forms of action and reason with "philosophic" forms. The first is equivalent to technique; the second, to prudence.

7

—␣␣—

When is Economics
Not Technical?

The analysis so far takes as given the claim that economics is a technique in the sense described by Aristotle and Aquinas. It is a method whose procedures are invariant to the ultimate ends it serves, and whose object is the realization of some proximate good. There is surely much truth to this assertion. Much of what economists do, when viewed in isolation from their larger purposes, is purely technical. Nevertheless, the previous chapter suggested that the complete isolation of technique from the context of the pursuit of a fully human life is misleading and dangerous. It is potentially harmful to the economist, who might dispose of the resources of his dis-integrated life differently if he evaluated their use from the broader perspective of his life's project. Even when economics is purely technical, it cannot escape moral evaluation in light of the ends to which it is put. A complete isolation also decreases the usefulness of economics in promoting human development, since it cuts economics off from broader considerations of human welfare. Finally, the fastidious repudiation of all connections to ethics in the name of professional integrity often leads to the exaltation of the limited ends of economics to ultimate status. This misdirection of economics impedes its effectiveness, even as a technical instrument placed at the service of humanity.

Thus, even when economics qualifies as a technique, it should not be completely isolated from ethics. In this chapter I take up the question whether this claim to technical status is justifiable, or more accurately, whether everything that economists do as economists meets the definition

91

of technique. Not surprisingly, the answer will be mixed; the important task is to locate the boundaries of technical economics.

As I noted in chapter 5, the word "boundary" is potentially misleading, because the realm of technique is part of the realm of prudence: the union of the two regions equals prudence, and their intersection equals technique. Technical actions come under the guidance of prudence, which determines the ends of technique. The question before us is not: When are we outside of prudence, and within technique? It is rather the reverse: When do we leave the technical realm, within which prudence operates at a distance, and enter a purely prudential realm, where technical concerns no longer govern?

To answer this question, this chapter will first outline in greater depth the differences between technique and prudence in the Thomistic tradition. In light of these differences, I will suggest four boundary markers for technical economics.

DIFFERENCES BETWEEN TECHNIQUE AND PRUDENCE

Aristotle (1941a, 6) provides early definitions for and an extended treatment of technique and prudence. Both prudence and technique concern themselves with contingent things—things that can either be or not be, and whose being can be affected by the person. Both are intellectual faculties whereby we achieve variable ends. It is their focus on contingent things that distinguishes technique and prudence from theory, which, according to Aristotle, explores those things that are invariable, like the truths of mathematics or the motions of the stars.

Technique concerns itself with making; prudence concerns itself with human action in pursuit of ultimate goods:

Art [technique] . . . is a state concerned with making, involving a true course of reasoning (6.4).
    Practical wisdom [prudence] . . . must be a reasoned and true state of capacity to act with regard to human goods (6.5).

Although it seems apparent that "making" is a type of human action, and is thus like "acting," Aristotle insists that making and acting are governed by separate faculties of the intellect: "In the variable are included both things made and things done; making and acting are different . . . so that the reasoned state of capacity to act is different from the reasoned state of capacity to make" (6.4). The two faculties are different in three ways; each difference will bear on our discussion of economics as a technique:

1. The end (or artifact) of technique is something external to the maker; the end of prudence is internal—the development of the acting agent.
2. Technically competent persons may perform their technique poorly on purpose and yet remain technically proficient; a prudent person will never act imprudently on purpose.
3. It is possible to be a bad (i.e., nonvirtuous) person and a good technician; a prudent person will not act other than in a prudent fashion.

The first difference between technique and prudence concerns the location of the result brought about by the two faculties. The practice of a technique creates something external to the technician: a material thing, a state of affairs, an argument, and so forth. As a result of the action of the technician, some *thing* becomes. By way of contrast, prudence brings about results internal to the acting agent; through the actions of prudence, *the acting person* becomes. Philosopher Joseph Dunne (1993), in an extensive treatment of making and acting, emphasizes this point:

> [Technique] has to do with making or fabrication; it is activity which is designed to bring about, and which terminates in, a product or outcome that is separable from it and provides it with its end or *telos*. Praxis [action], on the other hand, has to do with the conduct of one's life and affairs . . . ; it is activity which may leave no separately identifiable outcome behind it and whose end, therefore, is realized in the very doing of the activity itself (p. 244).

It is important to distinguish the sorts of becoming brought about by technique and prudence. On the one hand, the successful exercise of technique brings into existence something that did not exist before: a chair, or an argument, for example. On the other hand, through the exercise of prudence a person becomes more human, by participation in human goods. This internal goal of prudence may be confusing, because the person exists both before and after a human act; how then can a person become more of a person? To understand this development, we must relate human "becoming" to the nature of proximate and ultimate ends.

Recall that ultimate ends are not measurable in the same way that proximate ends are. We can measure proximate ends such as numbers of autos made, numbers of journal articles accepted, but we cannot measure ultimate ends like the quality of friendship or the degree of religious devotion. Ultimate ends are *principles of action*, not measurable goals, and their instantiation in a person's circumstances is highly particular. The internal work accomplished through prudence is a participation in ultimate ends; the external work accomplished through technique is some artifact, or state of affairs. It is participation in ultimate ends that constitutes the "becoming" that is realized in the exercise of prudence. Participation in ultimate ends is what we mean by the search for meaning in life.

Aristotle sheds additional light on the difference between prudence and technique by noting that, in the exercise of technique, the *form* of the artifact preexists in the mind of the technician, and is realized by him in his materials. By "form" Aristotle means the essence of a thing: that which makes the product of technique "what it is," the absence of which disqualifies other things as the product of the technique. For example, an account of those things that are necessary for a mathematical model of a labor market to count as a general equilibrium model (e.g., that wages and prices be determined within the model, and not be exogenous to it) is a description of the form of a general equilibrium model, its essence. Indeed, technique may be defined as knowledge of the form and the methods by which form is realized in practice.

Those who practice a technique can give an account of the form that they realize in the artifacts of technique. This knowledge of form is the product of reflection on the experience of making, according to Aquinas (1970): "For an art [technique] seems to be nothing more than a definite and fixed procedure established by reason, whereby human acts reach their due end through appropriate means" (p. 1). Because the artifacts of technique are external to the person, one can in a manner of speaking walk around them, observing and reflecting on them at a distance. By reflecting, in the light of experience, on the ways in which a particular end can be brought about, the technical expert formalizes the technique.

Because the form of a technique is realized outside of the person, the external artifact produced by technique is clearly recognizable as an end. A particular technical act terminates in the production of an artifact, the realization in matter of the correct form. Others who are trained in the technique can recognize and evaluate the instantiated form produced by the technician. Because the end of a technique is clearly specified, and is publicly observable, technique fits comfortably into the means-ends framework. When one comes to a technique, one need not deliberate about its ends; they exist prior to a particular exercise of the technique. Aquinas (1948, I–II, 14, 4) emphasizes the automatic nature of technique, claiming that the ends of highly developed techniques are so clear, and the means so fixed by reflection on the experience of making, that the technician need not deliberate even about the means of technique.

The operation of technique is not always so automatic, of course. Even while noting that many techniques need not deliberate about method, Aquinas allows that techniques which are carried out in highly contingent circumstances, like sailing or medicine, are not so automatic. According to Dunne (1993), in the practice of these techniques, the technician does not have the same control over his materials. Instead, practitioners of these techniques are "more readily thought of as intervening in a field of forces" (p. 254), and must be more attuned to the opportunities that contingent circumstances present. Within these more highly context-dependent techniques, considerations about the technique's ends become part of the technique itself, because particular circumstances may make certain ends unattainable.

For example, a physician may not be able to instantiate in his patient a perfectly healthy "form," and may have to settle for less ambitious ends. A good doctor makes his patients healthier than they are; he will not be able to restore every patient to perfect health. An important part of his job is the establishment of appropriate health goals for a particular patient, whose age, medical history, and responsibilities set limits on what levels of physical health can be achieved. Much of what economists do falls into this category of highly contingent technique. The constraints of data and the limits of mathematical tools force theorists and econometricians to decide not only the best means to achieve predetermined research ends, but to revise the ends themselves in light of research constraints.

Technique in its pure form realizes a given end in matter. Prudence, on the other hand, must both discover and instantiate human ends in the acting person. A person both discovers and pursues his ends as a human being through prudence. In the course of a human life, we discover "who we are" through experience, particularly through those commitments to action that participate in ultimate ends. Dunne (1993) explicitly contrasts form realized in prudence from that realized in technique:

> Whereas the [technician] can stand outside his materials and allow the production process to be shaped by the impersonal form which he has objectively conceived, the agent on the other hand is constituted through the actions which disclose him to others and to himself as the person that he is. He can never possess an idea of himself in the way that the craftsman possesses the form of his product; rather than his having any definite "what" as blueprint for his actions or his life, he becomes and discovers "who" he is through these actions (p. 263).
>
> . . . the function of phronesis [prudence] is not to maximize a "good" that one already knows and can come to *have*, but rather—a much more difficult task—to discover a good that one must *become* (p. 270).

Prudence is personal in a way that technique is not. In exercising prudence, the person directs himself toward his good in its entirety, as an integrated pursuit of ultimate goods. This good does not preexist in the mind of the acting agent. It must be discovered through action and reflection on the experience of acting.

If every technical act has a prudential component, since the person must choose to pursue through technique the ends of technique, then technique itself must in some way change the person who practices it. In its practice and accomplishment, the person must discover and instantiate what are thought to be ultimate ends—proclaiming that the ends are worthy of the commitments and sacrifices he has made to learn the techniques by which they are pursued. The technician to a certain extent stands behind the ends and methods embodied in the technique. An important question for our study will be the specifics of these commitments in the techniques of economics. To the extent that economics effects changes in the person who practices it, it comes under the guidance of prudence.

The first difference between technique and prudence, then, is that technique develops some product external to ourselves, while prudence develops the self itself. All of the other differences derive from this. The second is that, while technique can be done badly and still be technique, prudence cannot be done badly and remain prudence.

Aristotle's (1941a) formulation of the difference is canonical[1]: "While there is such a thing as excellence in art [technique], there is no such thing as excellence in practical wisdom [prudence]; and in art [technique] he who errs willingly is preferable, but in practical wisdom [prudence], as in the virtues, he is the reverse" (6.5). When we say that someone is *technically* good at a task, we mean something quite different than we mean when we say that he is a good, or prudent, *person*. Someone who is technically excellent has mastered a technique; the technique is his to command. The same cannot be said of prudence.

A master technician so combines knowledge of the form he desires to realize and control over the methods and materials of technique that he can successfully achieve the end of his technique at will. Those who have complete mastery of a technique can create even a poor outcome on purpose. A good flute player, for example, can play flat or in tune at will. The same cannot be said for a poor flute player, who plays flat when he tries to play in tune, and plays in tune only accidentally. It is the measure of control exercised over the technique that determines the excellence of the technique. A master technician will often produce poor examples of his technique as a way of teaching his craft to another. In economics, this is commonly seen in econometrics, where the results of purposely misspecified equations and properly specified equations are compared in order to drive home the dangers of careless specification.

A prudent person, however, never demonstrates his prudence through purposefully imprudent acts. To take the econometric example, a technically competent econometrician may purposefully produce flawed work; this particular action demonstrates technical competence, but it can only be prudent when it is taken at the right time in the right way, in pursuit of the proper ultimate ends. We have already seen an example of a situa-

tion in which a flawed regression serves a good end—the end of instruction. One might think of other situations in which it is prudent to produce
flawed regression results on purpose—to deceive an evil government
whose ends you wish to thwart, for example. It is not possible, however,
for a prudent person to act imprudently—that is, to produce a flawed regression at the wrong time, or a correct regression at the wrong time. We
do not call someone who acts imprudently on purpose prudent; we call
that person imprudent.

A prudent person cannot act imprudently and remain prudent because
one does not exercise control over prudence in the same way that one can
exercise control over a technique. We cannot distance ourselves from the exercise of prudence like we can from technique because prudence governs the
actions of the self in its entirety. Technique is subject to the will of the technician, and may be directed poorly on purpose for various justifiable ends,
including that of demonstrating skill in technique. Prudence, however, is not
something subject to the will, to be manipulated one way or another; it is a
characteristic of the will itself, expressed in the very act of agency.

According to Dunne (1993), the inability to be prudent while acting imprudently manifests a full engagement of the person in prudential action,
and a corresponding responsibility for one's self:

> In relation to one's phronesis [prudence], one has no discretionary powers to
> be exercised by some superordinate self. Here one is fully engaged and what-
> ever mistakes one makes must be put down to oneself; they cannot be as-
> cribed to one's lack of skill (as in the case of involuntary mistakes in techne
> [technique]) or to some covert intention of one's own which makes one mas-
> ter of the mistake (p. 267).

In the exercise of prudence, one cannot distinguish between possession
and use, as one may in technique: someone may have technique but not
use it (or use it improperly), but someone cannot have prudence and use
it improperly.

A technically competent person may purposefully produce a flawed
technical outcome in the pursuit of some other end. The flaw in the
technical outcome realizes some good: it is an aid to instruction, comic
or dramatic entertainment, or a demonstration of technical competence.
Because the artifact of technique is not good in itself, one can conceive
of a situation in which it may be made badly in order to serve some
higher purpose. The same cannot be said of prudence, because the end
of prudence—a fully human life—cannot be instrumentalized for some
higher end. There is no higher purpose toward which a flawed act of
prudence might contribute (Dunne 1993, p. 268).

A person's actions can only escape evaluation in terms of prudence if the
person is not held responsible for them as a person. Of course, this escape

from moral judgment (even by the self) is one purpose of modern technical discourse: it is a flight from moral responsibility for one's actions. Clearly, however, every technical act that is also a human act (i.e., is purposeful) can be judged simultaneously as technique and as prudence. The technician invests his entire self in the technical task, which is evaluated not only in terms of its proximate end, but also in terms of its purpose in the technician's life.

The responsibility that is assumed in prudential judgment highlights a third crucial difference between prudence and technique, first noted in chapter 2: prudence is a moral virtue as well as an intellectual virtue. Consequently, although one can be a bad person and a good technician, one cannot be a bad person and prudent at the same time.

One might dismiss this observation as the consequence of a mere contradiction in terms, a consequence of the way prudence is defined. Of course one cannot both do what one ought not to do and be the sort of person that does what one ought to do. If "bad" and "imprudent" are identical concepts, then one cannot be both bad and prudent. To dismiss the contradiction as a matter of mere definition, however, is to miss a crucial aspect of prudence: the distinction between use and possession, which is obvious in technique, disappears the closer one gets to the pursuit of ultimate ends.

The word "bad" is here an antonym for "virtuous." Recall that the virtues are human excellences that allow humans to achieve their ultimate end—happiness—through the pursuit of a constellation of ultimate goods. Someone who is "bad" is thus someone who has not developed the qualities that orient him toward his ultimate end. He will thus be unable to act toward that end—he will be imprudent. Neither will there be any further end beyond happiness that the person can pursue through imprudence—the possibility of imprudence being an instrument to some greater good is exhausted when the chain of ends terminates with ultimate ends.

The exercise of prudence demands the balancing of an array of ultimate ends, not all of which can be realized, in a highly contingent and particular environment in which various desires and difficulties compete for the will's attention. In this environment, a person's intellect will be unable to fully evaluate the situation for the person's will, so the will often must "feel" its way; it must be inclined toward the right action. The French Thomist Yves Simon (1986) describes the arduous challenges of prudence, and the necessity of a will attuned to the particular human good:

> But let us not forget that the specific duty of prudence is to tell me what to do no matter how unprecedented the circumstances, no matter how unique the situation. If the circumstances are common, perhaps I can look up the an-

swer in a manual and do what the book says. But in an unprecedented situation, which may be so constituted by the fact that there has never been a person exactly identical with my own self, as well as by the historical uniqueness of the circumstances in which I find myself at that particular moment, there are no answers to be found in any book. To know what I should do here and now, I must rely on the judgment of practical wisdom [prudence]. And this judgment, reasoned as it may be, is ultimately determined not by the intellect but by the inclination of the will (p. 96).

One does not simply learn to be prudent, although the intellect plays a role in the attainment and exercise of prudence.[2] Because prudence is both a moral and intellectual virtue, one must be trained as well as instructed in it. It is learned through experience of acting, under the guidance of someone who is prudent. We have already discussed the modern world's aversion to prudence: because one cannot give a complete, textbook account of prudence, it cannot be subjected to scientific scrutiny and formalization. As a result, disagreements about prudence cannot be resolved by appeal to a set of principles, but only by appeal to the judgment of prudent persons. There are no endpoints to which prudence is affixed; one is always in the middle of it, discovering and practicing it on the way, in the company of others.

The judgments of prudence involve all of the other Aristotelian moral virtues: justice, temperance, and fortitude. Justice inclines the person toward what is due to others in the community in which he acts: it safeguards the ultimate goods that are sought in community, and the good of sociality, or friendship. Fortitude protects prudential judgment from natural desires to avoid difficult or dangerous tasks. It allows the person to stick to a difficult course, which is thought to be in the person's best interest. Temperance safeguards prudential judgment from unreasonable attachments to pleasant ends. Like prudence, none of these moral virtues is completely formulable; one must learn them in community, through practice and experience, from those who are practicing the virtues already.

Prudence finds the balance in all of these virtues: keeping fortitude from becoming foolhardy bravery, keeping temperance from becoming crabbed asceticism, and giving due weight and balance to the various types of justice that are at stake in any decision. Because prudence in a sense manages, or is expressed in, all of these virtues, Aristotle (1941a, 6.13) claimed that all of the virtues were one, summed up as it were in prudence. Aristotelian philosopher T. H. Irwin (1997) attributes this unity of the virtues under prudence to the sweeping nature of the goal of prudence. Because prudence directs the person toward a fully human life in its entirety, all other aspects of human agency—both intellectual virtues (including technique) and the other moral virtues—are regulated by it.

In contrast to prudence, technique is not a moral virtue. The judgments of technique are not endangered by the passions from which prudence and the other moral virtues protect practical judgment. Although Aristotle (1941a, 6.5) observes that the passions may distort a person's estimation of the good in a particular situation, he notes that the judgments of technique are not similarly at risk. Aquinas (1948, I–II, 58, 5) observes that, because the product of technique is external, technique need neither bring about nor spring from moral virtue in the maker: "The good of an art [technique] is to be found, not in the craftsman, but in the product of the art [technique] . . . for since the making of a thing passes into external matter, it is a perfection not of the maker, but of the thing made." Because the narrowly defined goodness of a technique does not encompass the higher-order ends which technique serves, the goodness of technique does not depend on a well-ordered will, since the operation of technique is automatic, and need not depend on a will attuned to the good in contingent circumstances.

In its insulation from the influence of moral failings, technique is like theory, whose concern is unchanging truth. Just as one does not through passion conclude that the sum of the angles of a triangle equals 200 degrees instead of 180, one does not practice one's technique differently under the influence of passion or vice. An addiction to alcohol, for example, may prevent one from practicing a technique, but it will not affect the methods one employs in that technique. The alcoholic carpenter may be too sick to make doors, but he will attempt to make the same kinds of doors he makes when he is sober. His vice (addiction to alcohol) may have distorted his estimation of the value of drinking versus the value of being able to work, but it does not distort his knowledge of what is necessary to make a good door.

In light of this distinction, we can gather evidence about the technical status of any putatively technical task by asking how vulnerable it is to distortion from passions or injustice. An important question for economists will be: To what degree is the practice of economics affected by fear, desire, anger, and other strong passions, including the passion for justice? How important a role does virtue play in good economic practice? To the extent that economic research is affected by the practice of the moral virtues, it comes under the guidance of prudence, which regulates and sums up the moral virtues; the more directly it comes under the governance of prudence, the more directly do ultimate ends affect its practice.

TECHNIQUE AND PRUDENCE IN ECONOMICS

Recall that, in outlining the differences between technique and prudence, we are not distinguishing two separate acts. Because even purely technical acts come under the guidance of prudence, which directs them toward their proper human end, a technical act will have both technical and prudential aspects. Thus, we are not looking for those parts of economics where prudence does not operate; prudence is always at work, or at least it should be. On the contrary, we are seeking to identify those areas of economic practice that are not technical, areas which cannot claim even the limited insulation from prudential considerations enjoyed by technique.

The above analysis suggests four signs, or boundary markers, for economic technique. Economics stops being a technique in four instances:

1. When it cannot be done badly on purpose.
2. When a bad (i.e., nonvirtuous) person cannot do it.
3. When it affects the internal, human development of the economist.
4. When it addresses itself to a new field of inquiry.

The first and second instances in which economics ceases to be a technique are not directly relevant to the positive-normative distinction; they raise issues of ethical practice instead of ethical neutrality. We have already touched on the ability to conduct economic analysis incorrectly on purpose, in pursuit of good ends. A professor pointing out the consequences of common mistakes in regression specification, or demonstrating the limits of certain mathematical techniques by misusing them, is technically good, not bad. Likewise, a person who can carefully work out the implications of assumptions that he thinks are wrongheaded demonstrates excellence in technical economics.

When we move from the ability to purposely carry out technical economic analysis poorly to decisions about when it is appropriate to do so, we have left the realm of technique and are fully engaged in prudential action. The economist who conducts shoddy analysis in order to get results that his funding source likes may be technically good, and we may even admire his command of the subject, but his decision to purposefully misuse economics is not part of technical economics. In deciding to use economics in this way, the economist cannot claim to make a decision dictated by technique; his action cannot be judged solely in terms of its proximate research goals. No technical considerations intervene between his misuse of economics and the exercise of prudence (or imprudence).

The second instance in which a research decision leaves the realm of the technical is when the virtues of the economist affect it—when a bad (nonvirtuous) economist will make the wrong research decision. As with the previous instance, there are many instances in which the moral condition of the researcher has no implication for the quality of the research done. Any researcher can call to mind examples of colleagues whom one might not trust with one's valuables or young children but who are nevertheless valued for their technical expertise. That much of economic analysis does not depend on the moral quality of the economist who employs it is testimony to its technical nature.

The moral virtues of the economist come more directly into play in relations with other economists and policymakers, and it is at this point that the economist leaves behind the world of pure technique. The professional virtues of the economist encompass the classical virtues of Aristotle. Economists need fortitude (courage) when their results are unpopular or disturbing to colleagues, granting agencies, or policymakers.[3] Economists need temperance in order to resist the temptation to curry favor with the same groups, preaching to the choir in return for praise and high regard. Finally, economists need justice, in order to grant to the opinions and arguments of colleagues and students the respect due to them. Justice also provides the necessary balance of the rights of those in the communities that the economist advises.

The virtues are the safeguards of professional objectivity. A "bad" person is someone who does not have them, and is thus vulnerable to pressure from colleagues and others, or who does not treat them with due respect. Such an economist is more likely to distort his analysis, employing it to justify false results, or to use it to promote injustice. Disciplinary norms of openness and replication safeguard the integrity of the field against these vices, but no number of systemic safeguards can make up for a lack of honest, courageous, just researchers. Academic contracts and institutions cannot cover every contingency, or prevent opportunistic behavior in every instance, and neither can professional norms.

The first two instances listed above do not bring the positive-normative distinction into play; they are more concerned with professional ethics, and the moral virtues of economists. The third and fourth instances are directly relevant to the positive-normative distinction; they call into question the purely technical nature of much of what economists do.

The third instance—when the practice of economics affects the economist's character—is derived from the contrast between the internal outcomes produced by prudence and the external outcomes produced by technique. Actions that change and develop the economist as a person—beliefs, habits, and preferences, if you will—are not, strictly speaking, technical. Since economists are trained to see the world in certain ways, and to value certain aspects of social life over others, their training cannot be called purely technical.[4]

To see this clearly, we must distinguish between the effects of economic practices on economists who have already been trained, and their effects on economists-in-training. We must do this because the effects of economic practice on the person of the economist will be most evident as one becomes an economist—as one adopts the mind-set and values of the economic community. To focus solely on the established PhD economist when looking for the effects of the economic way of thinking is to miss the transformation.

A very small empirical literature has investigated the effect of economic education on the attitudes of students toward cooperation and altruistic behavior. Although these studies provide intriguing data on the attitudes and behavior of economics students, the literature is still too small and restricted to yield anything like an empirical regularity. Marwell and Ames (1981) find that economics graduate students are less cooperative in experimental settings than college and high school students, and interpret this as evidence that economic training encourages economists to free ride. Carter and Irons (1991) document that economics students accept less and propose to keep more in ultimatum game experiments. In this behavior, senior economics majors are no different than freshman economics majors. The authors interpret this to mean that economics majors are not made less cooperative by their training in economics; they are already less cooperative before embarking on their studies. Frank, Gilovich, and Regan (1993) contrast the increase in cooperative behavior of non–economics majors as they progress through college with the lack of change among economics majors, and conclude that economics prevents a natural increase in cooperative behavior. They also note that, although economists are less likely to give money to charity, they are no less likely to volunteer their time.

Of more direct interest is the survey work of economists Arjo Klamer and David Colander (1990), who examine the attitudes of economics graduate students throughout their training. Economists emerge from their cloistered graduate studies different people than they went in, with a new set of values. They tend to put a greater value on formal modeling and empirical methods. These values make it more difficult to take seriously concepts that cannot be easily formalized (like friendship), and which cannot be easily operationalized (like sorrow or spiritual well-being). A significant number of students more ardently espouse the benefits of free markets and free exchange, placing greater weight on economic desires which are backed up with dollars (willingness to pay), and accepting the proposition that "you cannot make someone better off by limiting his options."

It may be argued that these changes in values are simply changes in judgment. For example, the graduate student who comes out of a graduate program a free market economist may claim that the program did not change her values; it simply made her aware of the overwhelming benefits of free markets, and of the costs of nonmarket arrangements. This description is incomplete, however. It leaves out an intermediate step in graduate education—namely, the transmission of the evaluative frame-work itself. The economist who claims that free markets are almost al-ways more efficient than government regulation is working with a con-cept of efficiency, measured in terms of willingness to pay, which is in turn distribution-dependent. This concept of efficiency is itself one of the tools of economic analysis. Few graduate students bring these evaluative tools with them into economics programs; they certainly do not bring them into their first undergraduate economics class.

An economist is not simply someone who has mastered a set of axioms, or even a set of approaches to social reality. Someone who has "become an economist" thinks and values differently than her students; no one who has ever taught economics to undergraduates can deny this. Economics professors do not just accept their students' values; they attempt to change them through education in the "Economic Way of Thinking," which is more than just a "way of thinking." It is a habit that helps us to consider possible values and trade-offs that are often missed.

Economists should not be shocked by the assertion that they have values trained into them. Nevertheless, because they take for granted the values on which modern scientific inquiry and mainstream economics models are built, economists are often surprised to find themselves inculcating values in their students. This is shocking only to the putatively value-free economist, who may see it as an embarrassing problem, to be solved through stricter guard on the borders of technical economics. This values-purging is doomed to failure, and is counterproductive, because a community of scholars shar-ing a common inquiry and method will share values. It is more important to evaluate the purposes behind the values that a discipline shares than it is to pretend that it shares none. The values of economics (the normative weight placed on willingness to pay, the importance of formal method, parsimony, statistical significance) should be constantly tested against the ends that they are supposed to promote: understanding of economic life, advice toward the achievement of desirable social ends, and ultimately, human flourishing in society.

As we have seen, much of what economists do outside of the classroom satisfies the definition of technique. When the proximate ends are fixed—say, determining the male-female wage ratio in a certain profession, or calculating the subgame perfect equilibrium of an extensive form game—economists have a well-defined body of knowledge upon which to draw. In contrast, the practice of economics looks least like Aristotle's technique when economists develop new theoretical methods, or empirical analyses for new areas. This is the fourth instance in which we cross the technical boundaries of economics.

When economics is applied to a new area of social reality, there is strictly speaking no technique yet: both ends and means are indeterminate. True, the researcher knows in general what area he wishes to address (e.g., marriage), and he wishes to look at its economic aspects (e.g., its voluntary nature, its material consequences). Nevertheless, he cannot conduct his analysis in such general terms. He must define marriage, and posit theories about the nature of the commitments undertaken in marriage. If his analysis is to have any policy relevance, he must conduct his analysis with an eye to addressing "problems" in marriage policy (is divorce a problem or a solution?), whose resolution entails a judgment about what a "good" outcome looks like, or at least with an eye to helping policymakers and others think about the issues.

Groundbreaking work like this develops the field of economics; the discipline awards prestigious prizes and chairs for these sorts of additions to economic analysis. Yet these sorts of exercises, in which both the ends and means of research are specified, are least able to claim even the limited autonomy of a technique. The lines between "what economists do" and "what policymakers value" are most blurred at the frontiers of economics. It is here that Swedish Nobel Prize–winner Gunnar Myrdal's (1984 [1954]) seminal critique of unacknowledged value judgments has its greatest force. It is here that a fully rational justification of the theoretical assumptions and empirical specifications is most needed, to avoid the implicit assumption that the end of economics is "the ultimate end of all things."

It should be noted that, because established theories, like the theory of consumer choice or general equilibrium, were developed during the reign of value-free positivism, they are in some sense still on the frontier. Their implicit value foundations have not yet been fully explored. Bernard Hodgson (2001) offers an extended critique of the normative content of the theory of consumer choice under certainty. Walter Schultz (2001) offers a similar treatment of the implicit normative content of the First Theorem of Welfare Economics.

What sort of qualities come into play when an economist develops a new theory, or applies economic analysis to a new area of social life? Economic philosopher Mark Blaug (1992) calls the process of developing new hypotheses "adduction," and contrasts it with induction and deduction. Adduction is not formulable, and involves an intuitive leap from known facts and relationships to explanation. This concept of adduction can be reconciled easily with the concept of prudence; it is a certain intangible "something" by which good researchers come up with reasoned accounts in a new area.

Eugene Rotwein (1966) suggests that economists should acknowledge and discuss the qualities actually needed for good research, particularly the quality of "judgment." Judgment is needed when an economist comes up against the limitations of the mathematical approach. Its exercise leads to conclusions like "the assumption of self-interested, convex preference functions is unreal, but the loss in realism is compensated by the gain in analytical tractability." This statement is not a canon of practice; it is instead a judgment about the trade-offs involved in mathematical modeling. Rotwein describes judgment as an ability to be flexible, "a sense of proportion, . . . a habit" (p. 113). In other words, judgment is a virtue—one that looks something like prudence.

Economists are averse to discussions of judgment, according to Rotwein: "I suspect that the tendency to overlook this [judgment] on the part of some is attributable to the fact that 'judgment' at best appears to be something nebulous and, in any event, cannot be cultivated directly in a clearly defined way" (p. 113). Because one cannot formulate the rules of judgment (prudence) clearly, economists do not wish to talk about it. One cannot be "scientific" about it.

Rotwein's comments bear on the practices of economists even when they are not directly engaged in policy work. Faced with the limitations of their mathematical methods, economists must decide which aspects of social reality to include in their models, and which to exclude. These decisions are not technical; they require judgment in light of the goals "further up" the chain of ends that the economist wishes to promote.

Economic philosopher Fritz Machlup (1969) makes a similar point in the context of research that is more directly policy-oriented. Policy advice, according to Machlup, cannot simply take the ends of policymakers as given. Policymakers have a plurality of conflicting goals, and there are many ways to achieve each. Moreover, in the course of consultation, new normative issues inevitably come up. The policy economist cannot help but get his hands dirty in value questions.

> The inevitability of normative economics within (and not only before) instrumental analysis is a consequence of the impossibility of knowing in advance the choices that have to be made among alternative paths, alternative behavior patterns, alternative control measures. It is not just a matter of postponing decisions until we have to "cross the bridge"; it is rather complete ignorance of what bridges there may be to cross (p. 127).

Machlup, like Rotwein, notes that the qualities that come into play in the process of giving advice are not easily formulated, and are akin to what we have called prudence. The art of economics requires "a combination of human qualities that cannot be obtained solely from books or lectures. These activities . . . call for judgment, intuition, inventiveness, and imagination; they call for skill in making the correct diagnoses and prognoses required for successful prescription and good performance" (p. 107).

Both Rotwein and Machlup note that the closer economics gets to new fields of inquiry, or policy advice—that is, the farther away it gets from pure technique—the more it requires a set of less formulable, human qualities: imagination, inventiveness, and most important for our inquiry, prudence. These qualities are personal. They are not learned "from books or lectures." They are learned in the company of those who already have them, from mentors and colleagues.

Economists are reluctant to acknowledge the role of these human qualities and processes in the field. It makes the field too "unscientific," and will perhaps distract students from the hard work of developing the technical skills that ground the discipline. These concerns are not without force, but the neglect of the human factors has led economists to believe that technique is all that matters in economics. As a result, the field does not consciously value the means whereby judgment is inculcated in students of the discipline. It values "inventiveness" in the graduate school application process, but it does not seek to nurture inventiveness in its students and young faculty. This is not to say that economics departments are unconcerned with the human side of success in economics, but they are not self-conscious about the design of their programs toward this end. The field of economics would benefit from a more explicit recognition that economics training involves more than lectures, books, and seminars.

Economists regularly cross the boundaries between economics-as-technique and economics-as-prudence in their professional lives. At times the normative issues raised by these boundaries concern professional ethics: an economist is supposed to be objective, resisting the temptation to preach to the choir or to avoid controversy, and is supposed to act justly toward colleagues, students, and society. Moreover, an economist should act responsibly as an economist, using hard-won technical skills and particular expertise for good.

More often than they would like to admit, economists cross from technique to ethics in areas that are not covered by professional ethics. In decisions made about how to educate the next generation of economists, they train others to value certain techniques and outcomes, certain ways of making sense of social reality, that will affect the research decisions made in the field. In addition, when economists explore new fields, or advise policymakers in new areas, they cannot avoid reasoning about ends as well as means, because part of a new enterprise is determining what its goals should be.

This chapter makes the point that, although there is something to be said for economics as technique, it is neither possible nor desirable for economists to function as pure technicians. Economics is a human enterprise, and economists are only human. Most of us want to teach others to be economists, and to open up new fields of economic inquiry. Teaching and discovery are components of the ideal economics career. To engage in them effectively, we must make use of prudence, and traverse the field of ethics. The next and final chapter explores what this means in practice.

NOTES

1. Aquinas (1993, no. 1173) repeats the analysis of Aristotle.

2. Simon (1991, ch. 6) outlines what he calls "the Socratic mistake": the assumption that the question of action can be answered in purely intellectual terms, and that knowledge can be a complete guide to action.

3. The virtue of hard work is a species of the virtue of fortitude, and protects the economist from avoiding difficult analyses when they promise a greater understanding of an issue.

4. Polanyi (1959) notes that even technical learning changes one's identity as a person. We pour ourselves into our technical pursuits: "Every time we assimilate a [technical] tool to our body our identity undergoes some change; our person expands into new modes of being" (p. 31).

8

—⚭—

What Then Should Economists Do?

We should never cease to ask ourselves what we want and how we propose to get it.

—Frank Graham (1999 [1942], p. 29)

Summary chapters in books on ethics and economics are always dangerous. It is at this point that the author is supposed to reveal his program for a resurgent institutionalist method, a postmodern antimethod, a neo-Popperian falsificationism, or good old-fashioned positivist religion. I will not advocate any one of these alternatives; however, I do not wish to alienate any school of thought, and see nothing in my highly formal treatment to alienate anyone except perhaps a 1950s positivist (of which there are no doubt many). The Thomistic tradition offers a framework within which to think about the role of ethics in economics. I will be content if economists begin to reason within that framework. I am convinced that even a small move along the neglected dimension of human action will yield large marginal benefits for the discipline.

My parting thoughts organize themselves into three sections. First, the Thomistic framework suggests several pieces of practical advice for discerning the implications of ethics for economics, or more exactly, for integrating the economic project more coherently into the economist's life project. Second, one may argue within the teleological framework for any one of a number of research programs for economics. Third, the Thomistic project is really a plea for a more humanistic social science—that is, for a science of economics that is placed more explicitly at the service of human beings. This is not a claim that economists do not have humanistic goals already; the Thomistic framework simply offers a way to place those goals alongside the technical goals of the discipline in a way that reconciles the two, and puts them in conversation with one another.

SOME MODEST ADVICE

In the introduction to this book, I suggest that one of the shortcomings of the analytical critique of the positive-normative distinction is that it does not imply a program of action for the discipline; the logical analysis of the meaning of statements cannot of itself suggest what economists should do differently: If "is" and "ought" statements are different in kind, why should we care to keep them segregated? Why focus on "is"? In contrast, the teleological explorations of the last seven chapters suggest modest but real changes in the behavior of economists.

It should be noted that the Thomistic program does not require economists to seek masters-level training in ethics or philosophy. Nevertheless, they must examine their own values and the connection of those values to their work; this inquiry will bring them into contact with other disciplines, and a wider array of justifications and critiques of their work. It is a mistake to call this sort of project multidisciplinary—it is instead properly *philosophical*, not limited by the technical norms and considerations of any one discipline or groups of disciplines. The disciplines are supposed to serve this philosophical program of reflection on ultimate ends, not vice versa.

The most important question in this approach is not "What are you doing?" but "Why are you doing it?" Anyone who has ever had a three-year-old child will be familiar with the following scenario. A child asks why you are doing something—perhaps you are opening up the tool shed. You answer that you are getting out the lawn mower. The child asks again, "Why?" You say you are going to mow the lawn. The child asks again, "Why?" You say because you want the lawn to look nice. Again the question, "Why?" At this point the conversation is taking too philosophical a turn, so you say "Because" and end the game that so intrigues the child and annoys you.

Every economist should hire a three-year-old child to ask "Why?" about his or her work, over and over, until the economist has fully explored the chain of ends that motivates and justifies it. This exercise is easy, and may have surprising results. Consider, for example, an economist using regression analysis to measure the assimilation rates of U.S. immigrants (earnings growth relative to U.S. natives), by country of origin. The typical justification of this analysis is that it will help us to identify which immigrant groups adjust "poorly" (that is, slowly) to the U.S. labor market, and which ones adjust "well" (quickly). When asked why we (or a policymaker) should want to know which immigrants are doing well and which are doing poorly, the standard answer, implicit in most assimilation research, is that the information will help us to decide which immigrants should be allowed in (those who do well, presumably) and which to exclude (those who do poorly). Further questions ("Why should we prefer those immigrants whose earnings grow quickly to others?") will elicit a discussion of the benefits of immigration, of which natives benefit, and which natives suffer, and of the relevant empirical measures of labor demand elasticities, and so forth.[1]

At this point, some might assert that restrictions on immigrants, in favor of "successful" immigrants, are an unacceptable abridgment of the right of human beings to migrate (this is the position of Catholic Social Teaching, as documented in Yuengert [2000, 2003]). Admit the right to migrate, and policy arguments that tally up the costs and benefits of immigration to native workers and to government budgets begin to look radically incomplete. Policymakers must factor the interests of immigrants into their calculations. If a right to migrate, which limits the right of states to regulate the flow of people across their borders, is accepted, there may well be an effect on the research choices made further down the end-tree of research.

With a different set of moral presuppositions, the research may be subtly but significantly different. Instead of focusing on the identification of groups whose assimilation rates are low, research will attempt to explain why immigration rates are so low, and which factors can make assimilation easier. The substance of the research that has been done might not be much different, although it is possible that there might be a modest redirection of research toward those factors (enclaves, language, education) that might improve an immigrant group's typical assimilation profile.

Sometimes the economist's exploration of his own end-tree will result in a radically different research program, like the research into broader measures of human welfare in the development literature (see Sen 1999). Often, however, such a reappraisal will result in only a relatively modest redirection of research. Even when such an exercise does not result in a radical restructuring of technical concepts and measurements, the cost of the exercise is low; even modest gains in the efficiency with which scarce research resources are directed toward desired ends will justify the practice.

In certain cases, the placement of an economic research project within an economist's end-tree will reveal the unsuitability of purely positive approaches to the ends of research. A seldom-mentioned consequence of the neglect of the moral isolation of economic technique is that economic models are often constructed in such a way that they are unable to inform normative debates. "Positive" models, whose only purpose is to predict well or survive a statistical test, are often poorly designed to address the normative concerns that motivate policy debates. A clear example is the rational addiction model of Chicago economist Gary Becker and his colleagues (Becker and Murphy 1988, Becker, Grossman, and Murphy 1994).

Rational addiction models assume that addicts exercise complete control over their choices of addictive goods, and as a result are made worse off by policies which restrict their access to those goods. These models are justified by their predictive power—their ability to explain patterns in the data in a simple way. Unfortunately, it is impossible to construct from these models a normative case for antidrug policies that aim to benefit addicts by reducing their consumption.[2] A similar (but less extreme) difficulty arises in models of marriage and divorce, in which the costs of divorce depend on the theological meaning of marriage. The assumption that marriage is like a business contract may or may not predict divorce well, but its positive status cannot determine its usefulness for normative analysis.

Economic philosopher Bernard Hodgson (2001, ch. 6) points out a similar shortcoming of the single-minded focus on the "positive" performance of models: economists who evaluate and justify their assumptions solely in terms of predictive power and parsimony tend to adopt the same assumptions when conducting normative analysis. More specifically, Hodgson cites the example of hedonistic preferences. The assumption that consumers care only about their own material consumption might predict actual behavior well, and in a less complicated way than competing theories. The positive performance of the assumption does not justify its use in normative analysis, however. The reality of the assumptions may matter little when one seeks only to predict, but when an economist wants to use his models for normative advice, the realism of assumptions about human agency and well-being are crucial. Hodgson notes that economists are blind to this distinction, and fall easily into hedonistic *moral* theories because their hedonistic *behavioral* theories appear to predict well and are parsimonious.

Economists can be more useful to society if they will analyze more deliberately the human goods served by their research: the research questions that they ask will be more pertinent to human welfare, and they will have to develop models to address the normative concerns that people actually have. It is not enough to conduct research without reference to the ends of that research, hopeful that the research will happen to serve good purposes. We are more likely to achieve our goals as researchers when we reflect on them and direct our actions toward them.

The last chapter noted that decisions about the ways in which economists are educated cannot be purely technical, since they entail choices about what sorts of attitudes and skills to inculcate in the student. These decisions can only be made coherently in light of the ultimate ends of economic research. Those in a position to make curriculum decisions need to ask themselves what the goals of economics education are, and what sorts of experiences inside and outside of the classroom will move students toward those goals. Economics programs should also take care to produce graduates who have enough flexibility of mind to break out of the narrow confines of technique and to ask the larger questions that both determine the ends of technique and shape its substance. By doing so, they will produce better economists, who are both technically capable and able to guide their technical skill toward its most desirable uses.

Many economists fear that a teleological approach that refuses to lose sight of ethics will strip economics of all objectivity. The Thomistic approach does not require researchers to shed all pretensions of ethical neutrality; however, such neutrality is not defined in analytical ("is" versus "ought") terms. The inviolability of truth (one of the principles of chapter 4) protects theoretical and empirical results that are disagreeable to the researcher or to others. Moreover, an insistence on ethical neutrality serves a useful pedagogical purpose when students are young, idealistic, and liable to be carried away by passionate commitments to social causes. The French Thomist Yves Simon (1991) makes this point succinctly:

> An attitude of ethical neutrality, understood in a purely pedagogical sense, may be a wise defense against the eagerness of practical minds not yet convinced that the true rules of action have to be sought with much patience through indirect procedures in which the purposes of action seem to be lost sight of. The bad thing is that not a few professors fail to see the difference between a pedagogical indication and an objective necessity (p. 131).

Because the techniques of economics are difficult to learn, and its technical practice is arduous, the young minds who enter the field motivated by ultimate goals such as the relief of poverty, the promotion of social justice, or the development of nations must be taught patience. Many a graduate student complains that, immersed in equations and statistics, they lose sight of the vision that brought them to graduate training in the first place. Simon's pedagogical "attitude of ethical neutrality" encourages the student to master the indirect techniques whereby the larger questions can be addressed carefully, and to treat the "facts" and the technical analysis with the respect due them. Ethical neutrality is a *practical* safeguard of the value of truthfulness (Weston 1994); it is not, however, a theoretical necessity.

OTHER SCHOOLS OF THOUGHT
AND THOMISTIC APPROACHES

I would like to think, and see no reason to doubt, that there is much in the Thomistic approach that is congenial to many of the other schools of thought that have produced analyses of the positive-normative distinction in economics. Because the analysis here is so general—I do not make a case for one or another ultimate good beyond truth—the purposes and values of the various schools can be fit into its framework. I will not comment on every possible school;[3] instead, I will limit myself to brief comments on the postmodernists, the radicals, the Popperians, and what I will call the pragmatic mainstream.

Postmodern, rhetorical critiques of economics (whose most compelling proponent is Dierdre McCloskey [1994]) are critical of the modernist project, with its faith in an objective reality knowable by means of highly developed abstract methods (including positivist scientific method). According to the postmoderns, the modernist account of knowledge and inquiry is not credible, either as a justification of belief or as a research blueprint for the field. Economists do not really follow (and never have followed) modernist, falsificationist rules; in an attempt to show that successful economic research and writing is much richer than the "official" falsificationist version, McCloskey (1994) outlines the ways in which economists actually argue. Metaphor and simile, the well-told story, humor, and veiled appeals to authority figure prominently in economic arguments.

According to the postmodern critique, the positive-normative distinction serves the modernist project by maintaining the abstract purity of the discipline. The distinction is closely identified with the fact-value distinction, protecting economic "science" from contact with values that might cloud the clear view of reality afforded by positivist method. Since the postmodernists reject the special epistemological status of modernist methods, they are somewhat indifferent to and dismissive of the positive-normative distinction. It has no function in a postmodern approach, since value judgments are inescapable, and economic method should not close itself off arbitrarily to any mode of argument or inquiry that might persuade the researcher or the audience.

Because the postmodern thinker's seemingly offhand dismissal of the positive-normative distinction is so categorical, mainstream economists (who take the distinction for granted) have a difficult time taking the dismissal seriously. I would advise the postmodernist to reject the fact-value distinction but not necessarily the positive-normative distinction. The former is part of the analytical framework of foundationalism; the latter is older than modernism, and can be accepted without damage to the postmodern project. The Thomistic framework offers a way for postmodernists to continue to engage the mainstream without alienating it at the outset by rejecting any role for technique in economic inquiry. A positive-normative distinction that is based on the categories of technique and prudence, while insisting that technique cannot be fully understood apart from its context in a human community, holds out the possibility of productive engagement with the mainstream.

There is a curious affinity between postmodern and Aristotelian thought, most apparent in the works of philosophers Hans Gadamer (1975), Jurgen Habermas (1974), and Richard Bernstein (1983). In Aristotle's prudence, many postmodern thinkers have recognized an account of practical knowledge that is resistant to abstract formulation, which is learned and practiced in community, and which takes contingency and particularity seriously. Recent postmodern critics of economic practice may find fresh inspiration in the Aristotelian and Thomistic sources.

The various radical critiques of the positive-normative distinction (Amariglio and Ruccio 1998, Ferber and Nelson 1993) make common cause with the postmodern critique; the previous observations about postmodernism apply equally to the radicals. The radical critiques go beyond bare-bones postmodernism, though, seeing at play in economic rhetoric the structures and justification of unequal power in society. Feminists note the neglect of the special concerns of women in the use of terms like "economic man," and a systemic neglect of the value of the economic contributions of women, whose home and volunteer production are not included in national accounts. Marxists are similarly attracted to the postmodern paradigm, which provides them with a framework within which to display the economic interests at work in the shaping of economic discourse.

Those pursuing radical and postmodern agendas in economics can use the framework of this book without damage to their scholarly projects. Anyone who takes the Thomistic schema seriously will also have to take seriously the debate opened up by radical economists about what sort of society is desirable. The Thomistic framework will allow radicals to engage the mainstream on two levels: that of ultimate values like justice and equality, and that of the usefulness of mainstream models. Economists can no longer take refuge in technique from controverted, difficult questions of ultimate value and the social order. Moreover, because the heart of the radical critiques is that modern economics is neglecting important consequences of its method—the systematic neglect of the interests of certain groups—the radicals are in essence arguing that economic research does not efficiently achieve its ends: understanding and advice that will lead to an increase in human welfare.

Defenders of traditional, Popperian method can argue for a renewed commitment to falsifiability within this framework. It will not be enough, however, to invoke the fact-value distinction to specify exactly which sort of methods are scientific and which are not. This sort of categorization of statements by itself will only convince an economist who desires to be "scientific" but who cannot explain why being scientific will make economics better. Falsificationism will have to appeal to ends that are further up from its technical prescriptions, and the efficacy of Popperian method in achieving those ends, to make a convincing argument. To his credit, Popperian economist Mark Blaug (1992) makes such a case—he claims that a commitment to falsificationism will advance the discipline toward greater knowledge of the economy.

Although a Popperian can make his case within the Thomistic framework, Popperian arguments about method will not emerge from a Thomistic filter unchanged. The attempts in the Popperian tradition to sort out analytically the conditions under which a theory can be falsified cannot ultimately be successful. The insights of Lakatos (1978) about the ways in which researchers protect their paradigms from falsification, while insightful, do not generate a set of scientific rules for testing and rejecting hypotheses. When economic hypotheses meet particular data sets, the rules for the acceptance or rejection of theories cannot be hard and fast. According to the Duhem-Quine thesis (Quine 1951), it is impossible to test a single hypothesis; hypotheses are imbedded within a paradigm or worldview, a set of auxiliary assumptions that may be the cause of the rejection. The tangled relationship between core assumptions and auxiliary hypotheses cannot be sorted out statistically. An economist who must decide what to do when a hypothesis is rejected must use *judgment*, which like prudence cannot be formulated, but is instead developed and practiced well only in community, by persons whose habits (virtues) incline them toward right research action. That research paradigms cannot be accepted or rejected according to a set of comprehensive rules does not mean that the Popperian project has failed; it simply introduces into that method the need for judgment.

A fourth approach to the positive-normative distinction has emerged recently in the work of economists Samuel Weston (1994) and Daniel Hausman and Michael McPherson (1996). It is analytical but pragmatic. Both of these articles reject the fact-value distinction, but nevertheless defend the positive-normative distinction on pragmatic grounds, through an appeal to the desirable ends promoted by the distinction. I suspect that most economists who have read criticisms of the fact-value distinction take this pragmatic approach: economics is not value-free, but there are still good reasons to make a distinction between economics and ethics.

One strength of the Thomistic approach is its ability to bolster these recent pragmatic defenses of the positive-normative distinction by giving a more coherent account of them. Hausman and McPherson's definition of positive economics conforms to Aristotle's definition of technique: positive economics concerns itself with the production of "facts" according to a formalized set of values (ends). The Thomistic approach offered here specifies the advantages and limitations of the idea of positive economics as technique, and thus gives fuller shape to Hausman and McPherson's appeal to technique.

Weston's defense of the distinction jettisons the fact-value split in favor of a more commonsense, practical justification. His reasoning is entirely consonant with the teleological framework of this book, appealing to the ends of the discipline to defend the distinction between ethics and economics. After conceding the point that no economic analysis can be entirely independent of ethics, Weston offers four justifications for a positive-normative distinction. Three of his justifications are related, elaborating on the limited autonomy of economic science without denying the important role of ethics. The first is that the distinction keeps issues of the choice of assumptions (which may be ethically offensive) distinct from issues of the appropriate conclusions to draw from those premises. This is essentially an appeal to the usefulness of technique, whose operation can be evaluated apart from moral context. Weston's second and third[4] justifications for the normative-positive distinction are similar: the distinction promotes a scholarly environment, and promotes the norm of objectivity, by providing space for debating the truth of a logical or empirical proposition separate from its ethical appraisal. Both of these justifications express a desire to safeguard the value of the truths generated by the discipline. The positive-normative distinction is supposed to allow economists the space in which to ask what is actually the case, free of pressure to attain a particular answer in service to some end further up the end-tree.

In other words, three of Weston's arguments for the distinction assert that we should be able to argue that a proposition is true as far as it goes, before (or even after) arguing how far it should go. It should be noted that Weston's distinction grants economists some space to conduct "positive" analysis, but does not give economists a blank check to make statements about ethics. His fourth pragmatic justification makes this point.

Weston claims in his fourth justification that the positive-normative distinction serves as a caution about credentials. By separating positive issues, where an economist may claim some expertise, from normative issues, in which an economist has no special training, the distinction serves to warn economists not to use their authority as economists to promote ethical claims, and to warn noneconomists not to treat economists as especially qualified to comment on the good society simply because they can solve complicated calculus problems. This is essentially a plea for humility among economists about the uses of their results in public discourse.[5]

Economists have an incomplete picture of social reality. If economists do not know the difference between positive statements (about which they have some expertise) and normative statements (about which they have no more expertise than other earnest inquirers) they will almost certainly claim an authority in debates about policy that they do not merit, and they (and those who are impressed by them) will neglect important social and ethical considerations in their policy discussions.

ECONOMICS IS A HUMAN ENDEAVOR

In this book I have argued that economics should be self-consciously incorporated into the human project—that is, the life project of the economist. By doing this, the economist can resolve the tensions between the facts and technical practices of his discipline on the one hand and the normative values which are his explicit or implicit motivation on the other. By asking that most subversive of questions—why?—the economist will ensure that his work is geared toward ends which he thinks are good. He need deny neither his status as a moral agent, capable of reflecting and critiquing his own actions as an economist, nor his role as technical specialist; both can exist in a difficult but not impossible balance.

An economist who adopts the Thomistic framework as a way of thinking about what she is doing will find herself face to face with a set of challenges that are ignored by the mainstream positivist, but will find a new set of rewards as well. The teleological way is difficult, for two reasons. As a practical matter, it will involve the economist in a broader public conversation about the nature and goals of economics. The other participants in the conversation are PhDs from other fields, masters-trained popularizers, social activists who are impatient with academic critique, and public intellectuals who paint in very broad strokes. True intellectual exchange in this milieu is very difficult and frustrating; Daniel Klein (1999) compares it to "tutoring an ornery and spoiled child" (p. 8).

A second difficulty of the teleological approach is that it requires prudence, whose object is the complete, ultimate good, and whose practice is arduous for trained specialists. Decisions about action are always more complicated than decisions about technique, and require the courage and broad vision of a generalist. Yves Simon (1991) makes this point:

> No wonder that men dedicated to theoretical studies are reputed to be at a disadvantage when they have to be practical: their habits of thought are such that they have a tendency to leave out a few of the data or factors whose combination is indispensable for successful action. . . . It takes a great deal of versatility to be excellent both at the methods of abstraction, distinction, iso-

lation, and consideration in solitude which serve explanation, and the methods of synthesis, composition, and complex consideration, oblivious to nothing, aware of the significance of the most minute accidents, which are the ways of wisdom in the life of action (p. 8).

Economists who are trained in parsimony and abstraction appear to be at a disadvantage when questions of action arise. These questions require comprehensive vision, and an attention to the unrepeatable particulars of circumstance. No wonder economists would prefer to leave questions of action, and the values behind action, to others—to policymakers and other consumers of economic analysis. This abandonment of responsibility for deciding what to do is not an option for the acting economist, however, unless he is content to be a functionary of others whom he concedes to be wiser.

Although the demands of the teleological approach are great, so are its rewards. The ultimate ends of the discipline are what make economics most interesting, after all. Economist Geoffrey Brennan (1994) notes that all of the most interesting things in economics—economic efficiency, Pareto optimality, distributive justice, and individual sovereignty—are normative in nature, and cannot be addressed by pure technique. It would be a boring field indeed that excluded all considerations of higher-order goods.

One may admit the desirability of this approach to research as human action, and still wonder if it is worth the effort. Can specialist economists, who have had all generalist tendencies rigorously trained out of them, hope to be any good at being self-consciously generalist and prudent in reflecting on their research actions? Perhaps it would be better to be unreflective than to risk reflecting badly? Is an unself-conscious technical inertia better than a clumsy prudence?

This question must be answered negatively. Prudence is a virtue, and in the realm of virtue, Chesterton (1987 [1910]) reminds us that "if a thing is worth doing, it is worth doing badly" (p. 199). In this arena, imperfectly realized prudence is better than none at all. If economists were slaves, of course, we would not need to rely on their prudence, and would instead turn our attention to their masters. Since slavery is illegal, and even the most robotically technical economist must exercise some research judgment, we must depend on the economist to exercise prudence, however feebly.

Yves Simon (1991, p. 23) offers three reasons why an imperfect prudence is better than a technical abandonment of responsibility. First, someone who is trying to exercise prudence in directing his research is more likely to direct his research toward the good than one who does not even try. Second, the increased frequency of well-directed research decisions that will result from the efforts of economists to be self-consciously prudent is good for the discipline, and good for society. Third, one cannot learn to exercise prudence unless one attempts to practice it, however imperfectly. Since society is better off with more prudent researchers than with fewer, economists have to start learning sometime.

Most economists are already struggling to integrate the practice of economics into their lives as goal-oriented humans, even though the tenets of positivist method discourage them from doing so. By providing a justification for the integration, I want to free economists to do what they in fact *must* do, and are probably trying to do in any event—evaluate their research projects in light of their goals and purposes as humans.

A final observation comes from Thomistic philosopher John Bowlin (1999, p. 79), who notes that an important part of prudence is to know when to seek and take advice from others. The incorporation of an economist's research into his life's project is not a solitary exercise. Because human beings share a common nature (otherwise they would not be called human beings), they can learn from one another. Moreover, we are social animals, and we learn both intellectual and moral virtues in community. Because we share a common need for prudential wisdom, the humanistic exercise of economics requires friendship and community. Economists are aware of this, if only informally. We seldom seek out economic knowledge in solitude. The most successful economists share an intellectual life in common with other economists who are pursuing similar ends (in seminars, lunchrooms, and receptions). The pursuit of a humanistic economics has an important communal aspect, as does the pursuit of a full human life.

NOTES

1. See Borjas (1994) and Smith and Edmonston (1997).
2. Pollak (1978) and Yuengert (2001) make this criticism of rational addiction models. Gruber and Koszegi (2000) suggest an alternative specification of rational addiction, which incorporates time-inconsistent consumers (Laibson 1997, O'Donoghue and Rabin 1999), and which can be used to make a normative case for antidrug policies.
3. See Prychitko (1998) for a survey of the various schools in modern economics.
4. What I call Weston's second and third justifications are actually his third and fourth.
5. J. N. Keynes (1965 [1890], p. 76) and Sidgwick (1883, p. 24) also put forward the positive-normative distinction as a pragmatic limit to the tendency of economists to claim too much for their discipline, and hoped that it would keep economists from giving economics a bad name by overreaching in the realm of social policy.

Bibliography

Alexander, Sidney S. 1967. "Human Values and Economists' Values," in *Human Values and Economic Policy*, ed. Sidney Hook (New York: New York University Press).

Amariglio, Jack, and David Ruccio. 1998. "Postmodernism, Marxism, and the Critique of Modern Economic Thought," in *Why Economists Disagree: An Introduction to Alternative Schools of Thought*, ed. David L. Prychitko (Albany: State University of New York Press).

Anderson, Elizabeth. 1993. *Value in Ethics and Economics* (Cambridge, Mass.: Harvard University Press).

Aquinas, Thomas. 1948. *Summa Theologica*, trans. Fathers of the English Dominican Province (New York: Benziger Brothers).

———. 1970. *Commentary on the "Posterior Analytics" of Aristotle*, trans. F. R. Larcher, OP (Albany, N.Y.: Magi Books).

———. 1993. *Commentary on Aristotle's "Nicomachean Ethics"*, trans. C. I. Litzinger, OP (Notre Dame, Ind.: Dumb Ox Books).

Aristotle. 1941a. "Nicomachean Ethics," in *The Basic Works of Aristotle*, trans. David Ross, ed. Richard McKeon (New York: Random House).

———. 1941b. "Politics," in *The Basic Works of Aristotle*, trans. Benjamin Jowett, ed. Richard McKeon (New York: Random House).

———. 1941c. "Categories," in *The Basic Works of Aristotle*, trans. E. M. Edgehill, ed. Richard McKeon (New York: Random House).

———. 1941d. "Rhetoric," in *The Basic Works of Aristotle*, trans. W. Rhys Roberts, ed. Richard McKeon (New York: Random House).

———. 1941e. "Metaphysics," in *The Basic Works of Aristotle*, trans. W. D. Ross, ed. Richard McKeon (New York: Random House).

Augustine. 1961. *Confessions*, trans. R. S. Pine-Coffin (New York: Penguin Books).

Backhouse, Roger E. 2002. *The Ordinary Business of Life: A History of Economics from the Ancient World to the Twenty-First Century* (Princeton, N.J.: Princeton University Press).

Barzun, Jacques. 2000. *From Dawn to Decadence: 1500 to the Present* (New York: HarperCollins).

Baumol, William J. 1966. "Economic Models and Mathematics," in *The Structure of Economic Science: Essays on Methodology*, ed. Sherman Roy Krupp (Englewood Cliffs, N.J.: Prentice-Hall).

Beck, Lewis White. 1975. *The Actor and the Spectator* (New Haven, Conn.: Yale University Press).

Becker, Gary S., and George Stigler. 1977. "De Gustibus Non Est Disputandum," *American Economic Review* 67, no. 1 (March): 76–90.

Becker, Gary S., and Kevin M. Murphy. 1988. "A Theory of Rational Addiction," *Journal of Political Economy* 96: 675–700.

Becker, Gary S., Michael Grossman, and Kevin M. Murphy. 1994. "An Empirical Analysis of Cigarette Addiction," *American Economic Review* 84: 396–418.

Bentham, Jeremy. 1967 (1789). *An Introduction to the Principles of Morals and Legislation*, ed. W. Harrison (Oxford: Basil Blackwell).

Bernstein, Richard J. 1983. *Beyond Objectivism and Relativism: Science, Hermeneutics, and Praxis* (Philadelphia: University of Pennsylvania Press).

Blanchflower, David, and Andrew Oswald. 2000. "Well-Being Over Time in Britain and the USA," NBER Working Paper no. 7487, Cambridge, Mass., National Bureau of Economic Research.

Blaug, Mark. 1992. *The Methodology of Economics: Or How Economists Explain* (Cambridge: Cambridge University Press).

Borjas, George J. 1994. "The Economics of Immigration," *Journal of Economic Literature* 32: 1667–717.

Bowley, Marian. 1949. *Nassau Senior and Classical Economics* (New York: August M. Kelley).

Bowlin, John. 1999. *Contingency and Fortune in Aquinas's Ethics* (Cambridge: Cambridge University Press).

Brehier, Emile. 1965. *History of Philosophy, Vol. 3: The Middle Ages to the Renaissance* (Chicago: University of Chicago Press).

Brennan, H. Geoffrey. 1994. "The Impact of Theological Predispositions on Economics: A Commentary," in *Economics and Religion: Are They Distinct?*, eds. H. Geoffrey Brennan and Anthony M. C. Waterman (Boston: Kluwer Academic Publishers).

Bronfenbrenner, Martin. 1966. "A Middlebrow Introduction to Economic Methodology," in *The Structure of Economic Science: Essays on Methodology*, ed. Sherman Roy Krupp (Englewood Cliffs, N.J.: Prentice-Hall).

Carter, John R., and Michael Irons. 1991. "Are Economists Different, and If So, Why?" *Journal of Economic Perspectives* 5, no. 2 (spring): 171–78.

Chesterton, Gilbert Keith. 1908. *Orthodoxy* (New York: John Lane Company).

———. 1987 (1910). "What's Wrong with the World," in *The Collected Works of G. K. Chesterton*, vol. 4, eds. George P. Marlin, Richard P. Rabatin, and John L. Swan (San Francisco: Ignatius Press).

Coase, Ronald H. 1994a. "How Should Economists Choose?," in *Essays on Economics and Economists* (Chicago: University of Chicago Press).

———. 1994b. "Economics and Contiguous Disciplines," in *Essays on Economics and Economists* (Chicago: University of Chicago Press).

Colander, David. 1994. "The Art of Economics by the Numbers," in *New Directions in Economics Methodology*, ed. Roger Backhouse (London: Routledge).

Collini, Stefan, Donald Winch, and John Burrow. 1983. *That Noble Science of Politics: A Study in Nineteenth Century Intellectual History* (Cambridge: Cambridge University Press).

Crespo, Ricardo F. 1998. "Is Economics a Moral Science?" *Journal of Markets and Morality* 1, no. 2 (October): 201–11.

Croce, Benedetto. 1913. *Philosophy of the Practical: Economic and Ethic*, trans. Douglas Ainslie (London: MacMillan).

Drakopoulos, S. A. 1991. *Values and Economic Theory: The Case of Hedonism* (Aldershot: Asbury Press).

Dunne, Joseph. 1993. *Back to the Rough Ground: Practical Judgment and the Lure of Technique* (Notre Dame, Ind.: University of Notre Dame Press).

Dwyer, Larry. 1982. "The Alleged Value-Neutrality of Economics: An Alternative View," *Journal of Economic Issues* 16, no. 1 (March): 75–106.

Etzioni, Amitai. 1986. "The Case for a Multiple Utility Conception," *Economics and Philosophy* 2, no. 2 (October): 159–83.

———. 1988. *The Moral Dimension: Toward a New Economics* (New York: Free Press).

Evans, C. Stephen. 1977. *Preserving the Person: A Look at Human Sciences* (Downer's Grove, Ill.: InterVarsity Press). Reprinted in 1998 by Regent College Publishing, Vancouver, B.C.

Ferber, Marianne, and Julie Nelson, eds. 1993. *Beyond Economic Man: Feminist Theory and Economics* (Chicago: University of Chicago Press).

Finnis, John. 1980. *Natural Law and Natural Rights* (Oxford: Clarendon Press).

———. 1991. *Moral Absolutes: Tradition, Revision, and Truth* (Washington, D.C.: Catholic University of America Press).

Fonseca, Eduardo Giannetti. 1991. *Beliefs in Action: Economic Philosophy and Social Change* (Cambridge: Cambridge University Press).

Frank, Robert. 1999. *Luxury Fever: Why Money Fails to Satisfy in an Era of Excess* (New York: Free Press).

Frank, Robert, Thomas Gilovich, and Dennis Regan. 1993. "Does Studying Economics Inhibit Cooperation?" *Journal of Economic Perspectives* 7: 159–72.

Frey, Bruno, and Stutzer, Alois. 2002. *Happiness and Economics* (Princeton, N.J.: Princeton University Press).

Friedman, Milton. 1953. "The Methodology of Positive Economics," in *Essays in Positive Economics* (Chicago: University of Chicago Press).

Gadamer, Hans Georg. 1975. *Truth and Method*, eds. G. Barden and J. Cumming (London: Sheed and Ward).

Graham, Frank D. 1999 (1942). "On the Role of Values in the Work of Economists," in *What Do Economists Contribute?*, ed. Daniel B. Klein (New York: New York University Press).

Grisez, Germain, Joseph Boyle, and John Finnis. 1987. "Practical Principles, Moral Truth, and Ultimate Ends," *American Journal of Jurisprudence* 32: 99–151.

Gruber, Jonathan, and Botond Koszegi. 2000. "Is Addiction 'Rational'? Theory and Evidence," National Bureau of Economic Research Working Paper 7507, January.

Guardini, Romano. 1957. *The End of the Modern World: A Search for Orientation*, trans. Joseph Theman and Herbert Burke, ed. Frederick D. Wilhelmsen (London: Sheed and Ward).

Habermas, Jurgen. 1974. *Theory and Practice*, trans. J. Viertel (London: Heinemann).

Hands, D. Wade. 2001. *Reflection Without Rules: Economic Methodology and Contemporary Science Theory* (Cambridge: Cambridge University Press).

Hansen, W. Lee. 1991. "The Education and Training of the Economics Doctorate," *Journal of Economic Literature* 29: 1054–87.

Hargreaves Heap, Shaun. 1989. *Rationality in Economics* (Oxford: Basil Blackwell).

Hausman, Daniel M., and Michael S. McPherson. 1996. *Economic Analysis and Moral Philosophy* (Cambridge: Cambridge University Press).

Heidegger, Martin. 1977. *Basic Writings* (New York: Harper and Row).

Heilbroner, Robert L. 1973. "Economics as a 'Value-Free' Science," *Social Research* 40.

———. 1990. "Economics as Ideology," in *Economics as Discourse: An Analysis of the Language of Economists*, ed. Warren Samuels (Boston: Kluwer Press).

Hittinger, Russell. 1987. *A Critique of New Natural Law Theory* (Notre Dame, Ind.: University of Notre Dame Press).

Hobson, J. A. 1901. *The Social Problem: Life and Work* (New York: James Pott and Company).

Hodgson, Bernard. 2001. *Economics as Moral Science* (Berlin: Springer Verlag).

Hume. 1955 (1740). *A Treatise of Human Nature*, ed. L. A. Selby-Bigge (Oxford: Oxford University Press).

Irwin, T. H. 1997. "Practical Reason Divided: Aquinas and His Critics," in *Ethics and Practical Reason*, eds. Garrett Cullity and Barys Gaut (Oxford: Clarendon Press).

Jevons, W. Stanley. 1878. *Political Economy* (New York: Appleton and Company).

Jonas, Hans. 1969. "Economic Knowledge and Critique of Goals," in *Economic Means and Social Ends: Essays in Political Economics*, ed. Robert Heilbroner (Englewood Cliffs, N.J.: Prentice-Hall).

Keynes, John N. 1965 (1890). *The Scope and Method of Political Economy*, 4th ed. (New York: Augustus Kelley).

Klamer, Arjo, and David Colander. 1990. *The Making of an Economist* (New York: Westview Press).

Klamer, Arjo, and Deirdre McCloskey. 1998. "The Rhetoric of Disagreement," in *Why Economists Disagree: An Introduction to Alternative Schools of Thought*, ed. David L. Prychitko (Albany: State University of New York Press).

Klamer, Arjo, Dierdre McCloskey, and Robert Solow, eds. 1988. *The Consequences of Economic Rhetoric* (Cambridge: Cambridge University Press).

Klappholz, Kurt. 1984 (1964). "Value Judgments and Economics," in *The Philosophy of Economics*, ed. Daniel M. Hausman (Cambridge: Cambridge University Press).

Klein, Daniel B. 1999. "Introduction: What Do Economists Contribute?" in *What Do Economists Contribute?*, ed. Daniel B. Klein (New York: New York University Press).

Korsgard, Christine M. 1997. "The Normativity of Instrumental Reason," in *Ethics and Practical Reason*, eds. Garrett Cullity and Berys Gaut (Oxford: Clarendon Press).

Kuhn, Thomas S. 1970. *The Structure of Scientific Revolutions*, 2d ed. (Chicago: University of Chicago Press).

———. 1977. *The Essential Tension: Selected Studies in Scientific Tradition and Change* (Chicago: University of Chicago Press).

Laibson, D. 1997. "Golden Eggs and Hyperbolic Discounting," *Quarterly Journal of Economics* 112: 443–77.

Lakatos, Imre. 1978. *Philosophical Papers*, 2 vols. (Cambridge: Cambridge University Press).

Langholm, Odd. 1998. *The Legacy of Scholasticism in Economic Thought: Antecedents of Choice and Power* (Cambridge: Cambridge University Press).

Leamer, Edward. 1983. "Let's Take the Con Out of Econometrics," *American Economic Review* 73, no. 1 (March): 31–64.

Leijonhufvud, Axel. 1981. "Life Among the Econ," in *Information and Coordination: Essays in Macroeconomic Theory* (Oxford: Oxford University Press).

Little, I. 1950. *A Critique of Welfare Economics* (Oxford: Oxford University Press).

Lukes, Steven. 1996. "On Tradeoffs Between Values," in *Ethics, Rationality, and Economic Behavior*, eds. Francesco Farina, Frank Hahn, and Stefano Vannucci (Oxford: Clarendon Press).

MacDonald, Scott. 1991. "Ultimate Ends in Practical Reasoning: Aquinas's Aristotelian Moral Psychology and Anscombe's Fallacy," *Philosophical Review* 100, no. 1 (January): 31–66.

Machlup, Fritz. 1969. "Positive and Normative Economics: An Analysis of the Ideas," in *Economic Means and Social Ends: Essays in Political Economics*, ed. Robert Heilbroner (Englewood Cliffs, N.J.: Prentice-Hall).

MacIntyre, Alasdair. 1984. *After Virtue*, 2d ed. (Notre Dame, Ind.: University of Notre Dame Press).

———. 1988. *Whose Justice? Which Rationality?* (Notre Dame, Ind.: University of Notre Dame Press).

———. 1990. *Three Rival Versions of Moral Enquiry: Encyclopaedia, Genealogy, Tradition* (Notre Dame, Ind.: University of Notre Dame Press).

Mankiw, N. Gregory. 1998. *Principles of Microeconomics* (Forth Worth, Tex.: The Dryden Press).

Mansbridge, Jane. 1998. "Starting with Nothing: On the Impossibility of Grounding Norms Solely in Self-Interest," in *Economics, Values, and Organization*, eds. Avner Ben-Ner and Louis Putterman (Cambridge: Cambridge University Press).

Marwell, Gerald, and Ruth E. Ames. 1981. "Economists Free Ride, Does Anyone Else?" *Journal of Public Economics* 15: 295–310.

McCloskey, Dierdre N. 1994. *Knowledge and Persuasion in Economics* (Cambridge: Cambridge University Press).

McInerny, Ralph. 1992. *Aquinas on Human Action: A Theory of Practice* (Washington, D.C.: Catholic University of America Press).

———. 1993. "Ethics," in *The Cambridge Companion to Aquinas*, eds. Norman Kretzmann and Eleonore Stump (Cambridge: Cambridge University Press): 196–215.

———. 1997. *Ethica Thomistica* (Washington, D.C.: Catholic University of America Press).

McKee, Arnold. 1987. "Christian Economic Policy and the Role of Economic Science," *Review of Social Economy* 45, no. 3 (December): 243–58.

Mill, John Stuart. 1965 (1848). *Principles of Political Economy: With Some Applications to Political Philosophy* (Toronto: University of Toronto Press).

———. 1974 (1843). "A System of Logic Ratiocinative and Inductive," in *The Collected Works of John Stuart Mill*, vol. 7, ed. John M. Robson (Toronto: University of Toronto Press).

———. 1985 (1866). "Auguste Comte and Positivism," in *Collected Works of John Stuart Mill*, vol. 10 (Toronto: University of Toronto Press).

Mirowski, Philip. 1991. *More Heat than Light: Economics as Social Physics, Physics as Nature's Economics* (Cambridge: University of Cambridge Press).

Myrdal, Gunnar. 1984 (1954). "Implicit Values in Economics," in *The Philosophy of Economics: An Anthology*, ed. Daniel M. Hausman (Cambridge: Cambridge University Press).

Nabers, Lawrence. 1966. "The Positive and Genetic Approaches," in *The Structure of Economic Science: Essays on Methodology*, ed. Sherman Roy Krupp (Englewood Cliffs, N.J.: Prentice-Hall).

National Conference of Catholic Bishops. 1986. *Economic Justice for All: Pastoral Letter on Catholic Social Teaching and the U.S. Economy* (Washington, D.C.: National Conference of Catholic Bishops).

Newman, John Henry. 1982 (1852). *The Idea of a University* (Notre Dame, Ind.: University of Notre Dame Press).

O'Boyle, Edward J. 1990. "Catholic Social Economics: A Response to Certain Problems, Errors, and Abuses of the Modern Age," in *Social Economics: Retrospect and Prospect*, ed. Mark A. Lutz (London: Kluwer Academic Publishing).

O'Donoghue, T., and Rabin, R. 1999. "Doing It Now or Later," *American Economic Review* 89: 103–24.

Oslington, Paul. 2001. "Nassau Senior, John Henry Newman, and the Separation of Political Economy from Theology in the Nineteenth Century," *History of Political Economy* 33, no. 4: 825–42.

Oswald, Andrew. 1997. "Happiness and Economic Performance," *Economic Journal* 107, no. 445: 1815–31.

Piderit, John J. 1993. *The Ethical Foundations of Economics* (Washington, D.C.: Georgetown University Press).

Pigou, Arthur C. 1950 (1932). *The Economics of Welfare*, 4th ed. (London: MacMillan and Company).

Polanyi, Michael. 1959. *The Study of Man* (Chicago: University of Chicago Press).

———. 1962. *Personal Knowledge: Towards a Post-Critical Philosophy* (Chicago: University of Chicago Press).

Pollak, Robert A. 1978. "Endogenous Tastes in Demand and Welfare Analysis," *American Economic Review* 68: 374–79.

Prychitko, David L., ed. 1998. *Why Economists Disagree: An Introduction to Alternative Schools of Thought* (Albany: State University of New York Press).

Quine, Willard Van Orman. 1951. "Two Dogmas of Empiricism," *Philosophical Review* 60: 20–43.

Rabin, Matthew. 1998. "Psychology and Economics," *Journal of Economic Literature* 36, no. 1 (March): 11–46.

Radin, Margaret Jane. 1996. *Contested Commodities* (Cambridge, Mass.: Harvard University Press).

Rawls, John. 1971. *A Theory of Justice* (Cambridge, Mass.: Harvard University Press).

Reder, Melvin W. 1999. *Economics: The Culture of a Controversial Science* (Chicago: University of Chicago Press).

Redman, Deborah A. 1997. *The Rise of Political Economy as a Science* (Cambridge, Mass.: Massachusetts Institute of Technology Press).

Ricardo, David. 1953. *The Works and Correspondence of David Ricardo*, vol. 2, ed. Piero Sraffa and M. H. Dobb (Cambridge: Cambridge University Press).

Robbins, Lionel C. 1952 (1932). *An Essay on the Nature and Significance of Economic Science* (London: MacMillan and Company).

———. 1963. *Politics and Economics* (London: MacMillan and Company).

Rotwein, Eugene. 1966. "Mathematical Economics: The Empirical View and an Appeal for Pluralism," in *The Structure of Economic Science: Essays on Methodology*, ed. Roy Krupp (Englewood Cliffs, N.J.: Prentice Hall).

Roy, Subroto. 1988. *Philosophy of Economics: On the Scope of Reason in Economic Inquiry* (New York: Routledge).

Samuels, Warren, ed. 1990. *Economics as Discourse: An Analysis of the Language of Economists* (Boston: Kluwer Press).

Schultz, Walter J. 2001. *The Moral Conditions of Economic Efficiency* (Cambridge: Cambridge University Press.

Sen, Amartya K. 1987. *On Ethics and Economics* (London: Basil Blackwell).

———. 1999. *Development as Freedom* (New York: Anchor Books).

Senior, Nassau. 1938 (1838). *An Outline of the Science of Political Economy* (New York: Augustus M. Kelley).

Sidgwick, Henry. 1883. *The Principles of Political Economy* (London: MacMillan and Company).

Simon, Lawrence H. 1990. "Rationality and Alien Cultures," in *Midwest Studies in Philosophy, Vol. XV: The Philosophy of the Human Sciences*, eds. Peter A. French, Theodore E. Uehling, and Howard K. Wettstein (Notre Dame, Ind.: University of Notre Dame Press).

Simon, Yves R. 1986. *The Definition of Moral Virtue* (New York: Fordham University Press).

———. 1991. *Practical Knowledge* (New York: Fordham University Press).

Smith, Adam. 1985 (1776). *An Inquiry into the Nature and Causes of the Wealth of Nations* (New York: Random House).

Smith, James P., and Barry Edmonston, eds. 1997. *The New Americans: Economic, Demographic, and Fiscal Effects of Immigration* (Washington, D.C.: National Academy Press).

Vickers, Douglas. 1997. *Economics and Ethics: An Introduction to Theory, Institutions, and Policy* (London: Praeger).

Weber, Max. 1949. *The Methodology of the Social Sciences*, trans. Edward A. Shilz and Henry A. Finch (New York: Free Press).

Weston, Samuel C. 1994. "Toward a Better Understanding of the Positive/Normative Distinction in Economics," *Economics and Philosophy* 10 (April): 1–18.

Wilber, Charles K., and Roland Hoksbergen. 1986. "Ethical Values and Economic Theory: A Survey," *Religious Studies Review* 12, no. 3/4 (July/October): 208–14.

Yuengert, Andrew M. 2000. "Catholic Social Teaching and Economics on Immigration," *Journal of Markets and Morality* 3, no. 1 (spring): 88–99.

———. 2001. "Rational Choice with Passion: Virtue in a Model of Rational Addiction," *Review of Social Economy* 59, no. 1 (March): 1–22.

———. 2003. *Inhabiting the Land: The Case for the Right to Migrate*, Acton Institute Christian Social Thought Series (Grand Rapids, Mich.: Acton Institute).

Index

altruism, 68–69, 73–74, 75n5, 76n7, 103
Ames, Ruth, 17n10, 87, 103
analytical philosophy, 2, 8–10, 16, 64, 110, 113–14, 116
Anderson, Elizabeth, 25, 34n19, 62n11, 87
Aquinas, Thomas, xiv, 2, 9, 14–15, 33n5; faith and philosophy, 24, 34n15. *See also* Thomistic moral philosophy
Aristotle, ix–x, xiv, 9–11, 13–14, 22–25, 31, 34n15, 39–41, 44, 50, 54–57, 60, 61n1, 62n5, 65–69, 75, 75n1, 75n4, 78, 79–82, 88n2, 91–92, 94, 96, 99–100, 102, 105, 108n1, 115, 117
art. *See* technique
art of economics, 16n4, 106

Baumol, William, 76n6, 86
Becker, Gary, 34n12, 112
Bentham, Jeremy, 25
Bernstein, Richard, 8, 115
Blaug, Mark, 4, 6–9, 16n3, 105, 116
boundaries of economics, xiv, 5, 10, 61–64, 77, 83–84, 89n5, 92, 101, 104–7
Bowlin, John, 34n11, 34n16, 35n20, 62n14, 120

Coase, Ronald, 19, 83
Colander, David, 16n4, 85, 103
collusion, 74, 86
community of scholars, 7, 9, 31, 73, 102–4, 120
consumers of economic research, 15, 70–75, 77, 86, 119
contingency, 14, 27, 31, 34n11, 34n16, 55–56, 58, 63, 92, 94–95, 98–100, 102, 115
courage, 24, 99, 102, 108n3, 119
Croce, Benedetto, 15, 61n2, 62n8, 80, 86–87, 89n7

deontological ethics, 59
dialectic, 40, 46, 47n1, 48n10, 64, 69
division of labor. *See* specialization
Dunne, Joseph, 15, 55–57, 93–97

economic technique, 12; evaluation of the claim, 56, 96–97, 100–108; integrated into life of economist, 2, 49, 64, 95–96, 107, 109–13, 118–20; justification for positive-normative distinction, 13, 15, 57, 77, 91; limited autonomy from ethics, 7–8, 11, 50, 53–58, 63–64, 70, 78–81, 91,

About the Author

Andrew Yuengert is the John and Francis Duggan Professor of Economics at Seaver College, Pepperdine University. Professor Yuengert holds a BA in economics from the University of Virginia and a PhD in economics from Yale University. He has taught economics at Pepperdine for nine years. Before coming to Pepperdine, he taught at Bates College in Maine, and was a research economist at the Federal Reserve Bank of New York.

Professor Yuengert has made research contributions in several fields: labor economics, finance, the empirical study of religion, economic philosophy, and Catholic Social Teaching. He is currently the President of the Association of Christian Economists. He lives in Moorpark, California, with his wife, Elizabeth, and their three children: Rachel, Aaron, and Joseph.